IMMORTAL EGYPT

UNDENA PUBLICATIONS
MALIBU 1978

Invited Lectures on the Middle East
at the University of Texas at Austin

Immortal Egypt

edited by Denise Schmandt-Besserat

THIS PUBLICATION IS SPONSORED BY
THE ARCHAEOLOGICAL INSTITUTE OF AMERICA

Library of Congress Card Number: 78-53515

ISBN: 0-89003-056-1 (hard cover)

0-89003-057-X (paper cover)

Undena Publications, P.O. Box 97, Malibu, Ca. 90265

Mary and John A. Wilson
Chicago House, Luxor, January, 1953

As for those learned scribes . . .
Their names have come to be lasting forever,
Although they (themselves) have gone . . .
They did not make for themselves pyramids of metal,
With tombstones of iron . . .
Books of wisdom were their pyramids, . . .
Is there (anyone) here like Hardedef?
Is there another like Imhotep?. . .
They are gone and forgotten,
But their names through (their) writings
Cause them to be remembered.

Quoted by John A. Wilson,
"Egypt: the Values of Life," *Before Philosophy*

In Memory of
The Visit of John A. and Mary Wilson to Austin
November 12-14, 1976

TABLE OF CONTENTS

Photograph of Mary and John A. Wilson   ii

In Memoriam   iii

Table of Contents   v

List of Illustrations and Credits   vi

Preface - *Denise Schmandt-Besserat*   1

John Albert Wilson, September 12, 1899 - August 30, 1976,
    The Andrew MacLeish Distinguished Service Professor
    Emeritus of Egyptology, University of Chicago — *George R. Hughes* . . .   3

An Early Recording System in Egypt and the Ancient Near East
    — *Denise Schmandt-Besserat*   5

Perspectives on Irrigation Civilization in Pharaonic Egypt
    — *Karl W. Butzer*   13

Aspects of Egyptian Art: Function and Aesthetic — *William Kelly Simpson*   19

The Impact of the Art of Egypt on the Art of Syria and Palestine
    — *Harold A. Liebowitz*   27

Tin and the Egyptian Bronze Age — *Theodore A. Wertime*   37

The Garden of Ancient Egypt — *Leslie Mesnick Gallery*   43

Tradition and Revolution in the Art of the XVIIIth Dynasty
    — *Cyril Aldred*   51

Plates . . . . after p. 62

    An Early Recording System in Egypt and the Ancient Near East   I
    Aspects of Egyptian Art   V
    The Impact of the Art of Egypt on the Art of Syria and Palestine   VII
    The Garden of Ancient Egypt   XI
    Tradition and Revolution in the Art of the XVIIIth Dynasty   XXXIX

LIST OF ILLUSTRATIONS

Denise Schmandt-Besserat — An Early Recording System

Ill. 1 Jarmo: Spheres, Discs, Cones, Tetrahedrons; Prehistoric Project. Oriental Institute, University of Chicago I

Ill. 2 Ur: Incised Discs. University Museum, University of Pennsylvania II

Ill. 3 Susa: Bulla with its content of abanati. Département des Antiquités Orientales, Musée du Louvre, Paris, France II

Ill. 4 Susa: Bulla with check marks indicating the number and shapes of abanati inside. Département des Antiquités Orientales, Musée du Louvre, Paris, France III

Ill. 5 Numerical Clay Tablet. The Oriental Institute, The University of Chicago III

Ill. 6 Archaic Tablet. The Babylonian Collection, Yale University IV

William Kelly Simpson — Aspects of Egyptian Art

Ill. 1 Detail of scribe. Mastaba of Sekhem-ankh-ptah. Dynasty 5. Courtesy of Museum of Fine Arts, Boston V

Ill. 2 Detail of field-hands. Mastaba of Sekhem-ankh-ptah. Dynasty 5. Courtesy of Museum of Fine Arts, Boston VI

Harold A. Liebowitz — The Impact of the Art of Egypt

Ill. 1 Resheph Stela. Courtesy of The Louvre Museum VII

Ill. 2 Bone strips from el-Jisr. Courtesy of Israel Department of Antiquities and Museums   VIII

Ill. 3 Bone strip with running fawn. Courtesy of Israel Department of Antiquities and Museums VIII

Ill. 4 Cylinder seal from Ugarit. Courtesy of The Ashmolean Museum IX

Ill. 5 Military and feast scene from Megiddo VIIA. Courtesy of Israel Department of Antiquities and Museums IX

Ill. 6 Hunting for provisions, ivory from Tell el-Fara (South). Courtesy of Israel Department of Antiquities and Museums X

Ill. 7 Feast scene, ivory from Tell el-Fara (South). Courtesy of Israel Department of Antiquities and Museums X

Ill. 8 Samaria ivory. Courtesy of Israel Department of Antiquities and Museums X

Leslie Mesnick Gallery — The Garden of Egypt

Ill. 1 Conical shaped rocks in Japanese Dry Garden XI

Ill. 2 Great Pyramids XII

Ill. 3 Lotus Bundle. Lloyd, Seton, et. al. *World Architecture, an Illustrated History.* New York: Hamlyn Press, (1963) XIII

Ill. 4 Papyriform with triangular stem. Cénival, Jean-Louis de. *Living Architecture: Egyptian.* New York: Grosset and Dunlap, (1964) XIV

Ill. 5 Capitals illustrating different types of vegetation. Lloyd, Seton, et. al. (1963) XV

Ill. 6 God of Gardens, Khem. Wilkinson, Sir J. Gardner. *Manners and Customs of the Ancient Egyptians.* London: John Murray Press, (1854) XVI

Ill. 7 Hieroglyphic Group meaning Egypt, Wilkinson (1854) XVI

Ill. 8 Yshit Tree, Thebes: Temple of Rameses II. Lepsius, *Monuments of Egypt,* III XVII

Ill. 9 Garden in front of Tomb. Erman, *Egypt* XVIII

Ill. 10 Tomb of Osiris with Tamarisk. Wilkinson, *The Manners and Customs of the Ancient Egyptians,* I XVIII

Ill. 11 Festival of the Dead in Garden of Rekhmara. Maspero, *Mémoires publiées par les membres de la Mission Française au Caire,* V XIX

Ill. 12   Formal Garden, Tomb of Renni. J. J. Taylor & F. L. Griffith, *The Tomb of Renni*   XX

Ill. 13   Reconstructed Birdseye View of Estate of High Official. Charles Chipiez, 1883   XXI

Ill. 14   Estate of High Official at Thebes. Rosellini, *Monumenti Civili*, II   XXII

Ill. 15   Date Palm   XXIII

Ill. 16   Monkey Picking Figs. Lepsius, *Monuments of Egypt*, II   XXIV

Ill. 17   Pomegranate. Wilkinson   XXV

Ill. 18   Flowers on Floor as Decoration. Professor Sir Flinders Petrie, *Tel-el-Amarna* .   XXV

Ill. 19   Offering of Flowers. Erman, *Egypt*   XXVI

Ill. 20   Visitors being Received in Garden. Wilkinson, *Manners and Customs of Ancient Egyptians*, II   XXVI

Ill. 21   Vine Arbour supported by Forked Pillar. Wilkinson (1842)   XXVII

Ill. 22   Round Vine Arbour. Lepsius, *Monuments of Egypt*, II   XXVII

Ill. 23   Elaborate Trellis with Supports. Wilkinson (1842)   XXVIII

Ill. 24   Watering Device. Wilkinson, Vol. I   XXVIII

Ill. 25   Watering Device shown in Garden of Apoui at Thebes. Maspero, *Mémoires* . .   XXIX

Ill. 26   Vegetable Garden, Beni-Hassan. Lepsius, *Monuments of Egypt*, II   XXX

Ill. 27   Potted Plants in Garden at el-Bersheh. Newberry, *El Bersheh*   XXX

Ill. 28   The Palace of Merire. Lepsius, *Monuments of Egypt*, III   XXXI

Ill. 29   Palace of Merire; Suggested Restoration of Royal Villa at Tel el Amarna by Charles Chipiez, 1883   XXXII

Ill. 30   Trees in Individual Beds. Wilkinson   XXXII

Ill. 31   Small Residential Dwelling with Garden. Badaway, Alexander, *A History of Egyptian Architecture* (1966)   XXXIII

Ill. 32   Houses Surrounding Courtyard. Wilkinson (1854)   XXXIV

Ill. 33   Temple Garden. Wilkinson   XXXIV

Ill. 34   Dier-el-Bahari   XXXV

Ill. 35   Transporting Trees from Punt. Naville, *Dier el Bakhari*, III   XXXVI

Ill. 36   Cattle Feeding under Incense Trees. Naville, *Dier el Bakhari*, III   XXXVII

Ill. 37   Temple Surrounded by Trees   XXXVIII

Cyril Aldred — Tradition and Revolution

Ill. 1   Stela of Amosis (upper part): limestone from Abydos. In Cairo Mus. Cat. No. 34002. Photo from P. Lacau: *Stèles du Nouvel Empire*, Cairo, (1909) Pl. 11   XXXIX

Ill. 2   Relief of Tanent and Mont crowning Nebhepetre: limestone from Tod. In Cairo, J.E. No. 66330. Photo B. V. Bothmer, Brooklyn Mus. (No. L-452-23)   XL

Ill. 3   Model relief of Akhenaten. Collection Royal Scottish Museum, Edinburgh, No. 1969.377. Photo: Mr. B. V. Bothmer, Brooklyn Museum, No. L. 587.41   XL

Ill. 4   Relief of Sahure: limestone from Abusir. In Ägyptisches Museum Berlin/DDR No. 21783. Photo from L. Borchardt: Grabdenkmal . . . Saȝhu-Re, Leipzig, (1910-13) 11, pl. 17   XLI

Ill. 5   Jubilee Scene with Akhenaten. Collection: Fitzwilliam Museum, Cambridge No. EGA 2300.1943. Photo: Fitzwilliam Museum No. FMS 5381   XLI

Ill. 6   Jubilee relief of Niuserre: limestone from Abu Ghurab   XLII

Ill. 7   Akhenaten slaying an Asiatic—detail from the royal barge   XLIII

Ill. 8   The Royal Family. Collection: Egyptian Museum, W. Berlin, No. 14145. Photo: Mr. B. V. Bothmer, Brooklyn Museum, No. L. 539.14A   XLIV

Ill. 9   Torso of Queen Nefertiti. Collection: The Louvre, Paris, No. E. 25409 Photo: Mr. B. V. Bothmer, L. 582.5A   XLV

Ill. 10   Offering of an Olive-branch. Collection: Mr. and Mrs. Norbert Schimmel, New York, No. 107. Photo: Mr. B. V. Bothmer, Brooklyn Museum, No. L. 519.0a   XLV

Ill. 11   Stand of wheat. Collection: Mr. and Mrs. Norbert Schimmel. New York, No. 57. Photo: Mr. B. V. Bothmer, Brooklyn Museum, No. L. 521.36   XLVI

Ill. 12   Arbour with vine. Collection: Mr. and Mrs. Norbert Schimmel, New York,
No. 59. Photo: Mr. B. V. Bothmer, Brooklyn Museum, No. L. 521.62   XLVI

Ill. 13   The Goddess Selkis. Collection: The Cairo Museum, Tutankhamun Collection.
Photo: The Griffith Institute, Ashmolean Museum, Oxford No. 1088/95   XLVII

PREFACE

Immortal Egypt is the outgrowth of a lecture series on Ancient Egypt organized at The University of Texas at Austin in 1975-1976 in conjunction with the exhibit "Images for Eternity—Egyptian Art from the Brooklyn Museum." John A. Wilson, Andrew MacLeisch Distinguished Service Professor Emeritus at The Oriental Institute of The University of Chicago, was keynote speaker of the lecture series, and had graciously agreed to write the Preface of this volume. His recent death interrupted this latter project and has left all who knew him deeply saddened. *Immortal Egypt* is dedicated to his memory and in remembrance of his and Mrs. Wilson's visit to Austin.

I am most thankful to George R. Hughes, who knew John for many years as his student, colleague and friend, for agreeing to write a note in his memory.

* * *

The publication series entitled "Invited Lectures on the Middle East at The University of Texas at Austin" includes to date Volume I, *The Legacy of Sumer,* Volume II, *Immortal Egypt,* and the forthcoming Volume III, *Early Technologies.* The three publications are products of what we call "total projects," involving art exhibits and events to promote the maximum use of the collections on display, including lecture series or symposia, teaching activities, and community services. These programs received an enthusiastic response from the University and Central Texas communities. I am taking this opportunity to report on the various facets of the program built around the exhibit, "Images for Eternity—Egyptian Art from the Brooklyn Museum," in the hope that it might stimulate similar ventures in other communities.

The Exhibit

"Images for Eternity" consisted of eighty objects covering the whole range of Ancient Egyptian art, including some of the finest pieces of the Brooklyn Museum, such as the colossal head of a IIIrd Dynasty king; King Pepy II and his mother; a statue of Senenmut; and reliefs from Tell el Amarna. The traveling exhibit was organized by Dr. Bernard V. Bothmer, Curator, Egyptian and Classical Art of the Brooklyn Museum, and the descriptive catalogue was written by Richard Fazzini.

The Lecture Series

A series of twelve public lectures were scheduled for one evening a week. The programs harmoniously combined eminent scholars in Egyptology from the U.S. and abroad with faculty members of the University of Texas who had done special research on Ancient Egypt. A wide range of disciplines was represented, including archeology, anthropology, art, epigraphy, history, geography, Biblical studies, and architecture. The lecture series proved valuable in bringing together members of the community with faculty members and promoting a better understanding and appreciation of the material by the general public.

We are indebted to the Archaeological Institute of America, and in particular to Mr. Leon Pomerance, for the seed money the organization extended in support of the program. All the lectures were taped by KUT-FM, the University of Texas radio station, which plans to air the series locally and nationally.

Teaching Activities

While the exhibit was on display, a three-hour university course was offered based on the material of the collections and was open to all students of the University. The students, mostly undergraduates, came from a wide range of colleges in the University, particularly arts, general and comparative studies, communication, humanities, and natural sciences. The diversity of the class stimulated lively exchanges and most interesting discussions. During the two months the exhibit was on display, all sessions of the Egyptian course took place in the gallery. The students prepared for each class with assigned readings on special topics, such as "Egyptian gods," "The image of the Pharaoh," "Egyptian fashion," etc., which were then discussed in front of relevant material.

Students were required to attend each lecture in the series, and in turn, all speakers met with the class informally. These meetings generally took place in the gallery. I must say that it was very fascinating to hear the specialists comment about the material for which we were already well prepared and to be able to ask them the many questions we had. I was very pleased that the lecturers also seemed to enjoy the contact with the students and commented favorably on their eagerness to learn, their attentiveness, and the quality of their questions. As a teacher, I was pleased at how all the information gathered in the exhibit and during the lectures was meaningfully integrated by the students in their term papers. They were required to study in depth three artifacts of the exhibit. Many were seen spending long hours in the galleries studying all facets of the artifacts they had selected. Most of the papers showed keen personal observations which could never have been made from photographs and which also referred to comments made by speakers which could not be found in books.

In my opinion, the course on Egypt was ideal; it involved a meaningful assemblage of splendid material, some of the best scholars in the field, and a group of bright and interested students who realized the uniqueness of the experience and communicated to the course a special enthusiasm throughout the semester.

I am grateful to all those who have made this project possible: in particular, Donald B. Goodall, Director of Collections, and Marian B. Davis, Chief Curator of the University of Texas Art Museum; Irwin C. Lieb, Vice-President and Dean of Graduate Studies; and Elspeth D. Rostow, Dean of General and Comparative Studies. In addition, I owe a special thanks to Paul W. English, Director of the Center for Middle Eastern Studies, and his staff, who so graciously helped accomplish innumerable tasks during all phases of the project, and also to Ralph J. Kaufmann, Chairman of the Comparative Studies Program, who realized the teaching potential of the event and sponsored the course.

Of course, the greatest credit should be given to the Brooklyn Museum and in particular to Dr. Bernard V. Bothmer who took the initiative to organize the traveling exhibit and to share their finest pieces with other museums. We felt it was a great personal opportunity for us, and hope that this volume will carry the benefit of the experience to others.

Denise Schmandt-Besserat
Coordinator
Assistant Professor of Art

John Albert Wilson
September 12, 1899 - August 30, 1976
The Andrew MacLeish Distinguished Service Professor Emeritus
of Egyptology, University of Chicago

by

George R. Hughes

John A. Wilson was for over a quarter of a century the doyen of American Egyptologists and had become perhaps the best known of all the world's Egyptologists. His work commanded the respect of his peers in Egyptology and was constantly cited by reason of its firm scholarly basis. His province was largely the texts, hieroglyphic and hieratic, surviving from ancient Egypt. He was a strict grammarian and lexicographer, hewing assiduously to the line in his translations of the texts. Yet he was a historian first and foremost, and not only a historian of the political career of Egypt but of its social, economic and religious development as well. He was chiefly interested in the history of ideas in pharaonic times.

Wilson's bibliography contains many articles on a wide variety of facets of ancient Egyptian civilization, many of them dealing with the basic translation and interpretation of texts. It was from such first-hand reading and re-reading of the pertinent texts that he produced his three-chapter essay on ancient Egyptian speculative thought in *The Intellectual Adventure of Ancient Man* (1946), which appeared also in a paperback edition entitled *Before Philosophy* (1949).

Despite Wilson's fascination with and flair for searching out the expressions of ideas and for tracing the change and development of them through time, probably his most widely used work is his translation of the Egyptian texts of various sorts that appear in *Ancient Near Eastern Texts Relating to the Old Testament* (1950), which has undergone two revisions (1955 and 1969). His translations of these texts are constantly used by scholars and students of the ancient Near East, but they are just as frequently appealed to by Egyptologists themselves. In a similar manner, the book that was Wilson's most significant contribution to Egyptology, *The Burden of Egypt: An Interpretation of Ancient Egyptian Culture* (1951), is not only a *vade mecum* for the Egyptologist; its readability has made its appeal a wide one. It was re-issued in paperback under the title *The Culture of Ancient Egypt* (1956) and has been translated into Arabic, French, German, Italian and Spanish. Part of its appeal to serious students derives from its different approach. As Wilson wrote in the introduction to it: "This is not a history of ancient Egypt, but rather a book about ancient Egyptian history," a first attempt to assess "the significance and 'value' of the story." His ability to state clearly, incisively and attractively, which made these scholarly treatises readable, also made him an exceptional class-room teacher, a highly successful lecturer to general audiences, and a sought-after contributor to widely diversified journals. He was for much of his career the unofficial spokesman for American Egyptology. His *Signs and Wonders Upon Pharaoh* (1964), a history of American Egyptology, which he said he had greatly enjoyed writing, and his autobiography, *Thousands of Years* (1972), are eminently readable and engaging because he had a sense of the amusing, the incongruous and the dramatic in the events he described, whether they occurred in antiquity or in his own experience.

The qualities that distinguished him as a scholar also placed him in great demand from about 1950 on as a counsellor and member of committees, both national and international, in learned societies and on governmental commissions. When the new High Dam at Aswān was to be built, it was he who was gotten to be the American member and eventually chairman of the UNESCO Consultative Committee for the Salvage of the Nubian Monuments. So great was the demand upon his time that at one point at the height of his involvement on many fronts he was to complain that he had become "only a stuffed shirt." But it was precisely because he applied the same acumen and orderliness of mind to organizational matters as he did to Egyptian texts that he was found to be a useful advisor and consultant.

When Wilson graduated form Princeton in 1920 he expected to go on to graduate study, perhaps in Eastern European history, but he needed money for that so he accepted a three-year teaching post at what later became the American University of Beirut in Lebanon. He taught English there and came to know a longtime faculty member, Harold H. Nelson, who had taken a doctorate in Egyptology under James H. Breasted at the University of Chicago. Nelson introduced Wilson to Egyptian hieroglyphs and also to Breasted, who visited Beirut in the spring of 1923. Upon Nelson's recommendation Breasted offered Wilson, who had become fascinated with ancient Egypt on a 1922 trip up the Nile, a fellowship in his new Oriental Institute. Wilson came to Chicago in 1923, earned his doctorate in 1926, and was sent as an epigraphist to Luxor, Egypt, on the staff of the also new Epigraphic Survey, the director of which was Harold H. Nelson. In 1931 Wilson returned to Chicago to the faculty as a visiting assistant professor. In 1936, upon Breasted's death, he succeeded to the directorship of the Oriental Institute and continued as Director until 1946 through the most difficult of financial times for the Institute. In 1953 he was honored by being named a Distinguished Service Professor in the University.

Among the many honors conferred upon him by American and foreign societies and universities were a D. Litt. by his *alma mater*, Princeton, in 1961 and a D.H.L. by Loyola University of Chicago in 1974. He was elected a corresponding member of the German Archaeological Institute in 1937, a member of the American Philosophical Society in 1954 and of the American Academy of Arts and Sciences in 1968, and a corresponding member of the Institut d'Egypte in 1969. Perhaps the most extraordinary of all these honors was the establishment, by the gift of an admirer, of the John A. Wilson Professorship of Oriental Studies in the University of Chicago in 1968 on the eve of his becoming *emeritus*. Finally, on his seventieth birthday in 1969 his colleagues and former students presented him with a volume, *Studies in Honor of John A. Wilson*.

John Wilson was above all else a precise and exacting scholar who made a large and lasting contribution to Egyptian studies, and that was the basis of all the demands upon him and all the honors that came to him.

An Early Recording System
in Egypt and the Ancient Near East*

by

Denise Schmandt-Besserat
The University of Texas at Austin

I. Introduction

In 1969-71 I received a fellowship from the Radcliffe Institute to investigate the beginnings of the uses of clay by man in the Middle East.[1] Among the earliest clay artifacts I observed was a group of minute objects that began to appear *ca.* 8500 B.C. and were formed into geometric shapes, including spheres, discs, cones, tetrahedrons and cylindrical rods (Ill. 1). I called them "geometric objects" and found them very intriguing because their use was unknown; but their specific shapes, the great care with which some were manufactured, and their abundance suggests a function of some importance. I began looking for them in site reports and collections and soon discovered that they are virtually omnipresent and that rare are the Middle Eastern sites dating between the IXth and IIrd millennium B.C. in which they do not occur. I had assumed that they were solely a Western Asiatic phenomenon until the arrival in Austin of an exhibit of Egyptian art, *Images for Eternity*, which gave me the opportunity to teach a course on Egypt. For my class preparation I went back to early site reports and was greatly surprised to find the same geometric tokens in Egypt and in particular at Khartoum[2] and Abydos.[3] The heading under which they are published in the Khartoum report, "small objects of uncertain purposes," indicates that they are also a puzzle to Egyptologists. I would like to take this opportunity to report how it became evident that the "geometric objects" were used as counters (Akkadian: *abnu*, pl. *abnati*) in an early archaic system of recording.[4] I will attempt in this paper to (1) describe the abnati system; (2) show how it evolved into writing; and (3) draw some of the implications of the fact that Egypt and the Near East may have shared a prewriting recording system.

II. The Abnati System of Recording

The abnati are of many shapes. There are spheres, discs, cones, tetrahedrons, cylinders, and many shapes that are very difficult to describe because they are so odd. The various types come in various sizes, which, although

*This article is the result of a study sponsored by the Radcliffe Institute in 1969-71 and a travel grant to study early clay collections in the Middle East by the Wenner-Gren Foundation (grant no. 2684, 1970).

[1] Denise Schmandt-Besserat. "The Use of Clay before Pottery in the Zagros," *Expedition*, Vol. 16, No. 2, 1974; "The Earliest Uses of Clay in Syria," *Expedition*, Vol. 19, No. 3, 1977; and "The Earliest Uses of Clay in Turkey," *Anatolian Studies*, Vol. 27, 1977.

[2] A. J. Arkell. *Early Khartoum*, Oxford University Press, 1949, p. 79ff.

[3] Walter B. Emery. *Great Tombs of the First Dynasty*, Vol. II, Egypt Exploration Society, Oxford University Press, 1954, p. 56-59.

[4] Denise Schmandt-Besserat. "An Archaic Recording System and the Origin of Writing," *Syro-Mesopotamian Studies*, Vol. I, Issue 2, July 1977.

not standardized, may have had a meaning. There is also a series of objects in each type that bear various incised and punched markings (Ill. 2).

The abnati reported in Khartoum are of two types: spheres and discs. There are 16 spheres, which vary in size from 5 mm to 26 mm in diameter. Another group of 10 spheres bear incised markings. They vary from 18 mm to 37 mm and have one or several deep grooves. There are also 49 spheres at Abydos, measuring *ca.* 10 mm. The second shape represented at Khartoum are discs; all of them have incised markings. Seven discs have a nick in the rim, five others have two nicks at roughly opposite sides on the rim, and two final examples bear one groove on the surface of one face.

The abnati assemblages of both Khartoum and Abydos are poor compared to most sites of the Middle East, where at least the four basic types of abnati are generally represented. For instance, an assemblage of 219 abnati, which includes 20 various shapes and dates back to the IXth millennium in Iran, was found at Tepe Asiab.[5]

The abnati found in Khartoum are made with very little care and present coarse surfaces and very irregular shapes. On the other hand, most of the Abydos examples are very carefully made. The majority of the abnati are made of clay and are modelled with the hands, either by rolling them between the palms or pinching them with the finger tips. Their color, which ranges from buff to red with many blackish examples, suggests that light firing was involved. A few examples in the Middle East are made of various stones, but all the examples reported at Abydos are made of either limestone, steatite, or alabaster.

Tepe Asiab[6] and Ganj-i-Dareh Tepe[7] in Iran as well as Beldibi[8] in Turkey are the earliest sites where abnati are presently known to occur in the Middle East (chart 1). The three sites are contemporary and may be dated to the middle of the IXth millennium B.C. (Ganj Dareh Tepe Level E 8450±150 B.C., GAK 807). The wide distribution of abnati suggests that, at that time, the abnati system was already well known. The abnati become virtually ubiquitous in the Middle East in the VIIth millennium B.C. and are, for instance, represented in the Neolithic sites of Khartoum (Nubia), Jericho (Palestine), Tell Ramad (Syria), Jarmo (Iraq), and Anau (Iran). They continue to be found in Chalcolithic assemblages, for example, at Tell Arpachiya, Tell-as-Sawwan, and Tal-i-Iblis. In the Bronze Age they occur in the Mesopotamian urban centers of Ur, Tello, Fara, Uruk, Kish, Je...det Nasr, as well as in Egypt at Abydos, and in the Indus Valley at Chanhu Daro, thus including all the major Near Eastern civilizations of the time.

The small tokens are often discussed in site reports, but they seem to have escaped special attention of archaeologists because they are usually reported under various headings. The cones are sometimes incorporated with the figurines, the spheres with "games", and the rest under headings such as "small objects of uncertain purposes." They are never seen as belonging together. At Abydos, the spheres are classified under the heading "games," but Emery does mention the possibility of their being counters.[9] The number of the geometric tokens at each site may reach sizeable proportions; for instance, the Jarmo report mentions 1153 spheres, 206 discs, and 106 cones.[10]

When I started collecting data about the clay tokens, I was asked by many archaeologists what they represented. The answer to the question was to be found in the work of two scholars: A. Leo Oppenheim, of

---

[5]Collections of the Prehistoric Project, The Oriental Institute, The University of Chicago.

[6]R. J. Braidwood, Bruce Howe, Charles A. Reed. "The Iranian Prehistoric Project," *Science,* June 23, 1961, Vol. 133, No. 3469, pp. 2008-10.

[7]P. E. L. Smith. "Survey of Excavations: Ganj-Dareh Tepe," *Iran,* Vol. VIII, pp. 174-76, 1970.

[8]E. Bostanci. "Beldibi ve Magracikta Yapilam 1967 yaz Mavsimi Kazilari ve Yeni Buluntular," *Turk Arkeoloji Dergisi,* Vol. XVI, I, 1968, p. 58, Fig. 3.

[9]W. B. Emery, *op. cit.,* p. 56.

[10]Vivian L. Broman. *Jarmo Figurines.* Unpublished Master's Thesis, Harvard University-Peabody Museum Library, Cambridge, Mass., 1958. pp. 62, 63, 58.

the Oriental Institute of the University of Chicago, and Pierre Amiet, of the Musée du Louvre, Paris. In 1958, Oppenheim described an interesting accounting system based on tokens used to keep count of the animals in the herds of the palace of Nuzi.[11] Each animal was represented by an abnu and deposited in a basket. Abnati would be transferred to appropriate baskets to keep track of change of pasture or shepherds, when animals were shorn, etc. Oppenheim was able to deduce this information by the presence of short notes written in cuneiform script on clay tablets, all referring to "abnati". They mentioned, for instance, that abnati had been "deposited" or "transferred" or "removed." In the same context, a singular tablet was found that was hollow and contained 48 abnati corresponding to a list in cuneiform script written on the surface of the tablet enumerating various animals including rams, ewes, kids, sheep, etc. and totalling to 48. The hollow tablet was found intact in excavations and was carefully opened to check the content. The abnati found inside were the first tangible evidence found of a system of accounting based on tokens. The hollow tablet probably represents a transfer of abnati from one service of the palace to the other, such as mentioned on the short notes.

The findings of Nuzi allowed Pierre Amiet to understand the significance of a series of hollow clay balls (bulla, pl. bullae) filled with small tokens found at Susa and dated to about 3100 B.C. (Ill. 3).[12] As the Susa bullae predated writing, they bear no inscription except cylinder seal impressions rolled upon their surface, which attested to their official use. Amiet identified the clay balls as devices similar to the Nuzi hollow tablet and he identified the small objects inside as counters. The Susa bullae, therefore, produced the first abnati available to study, following the loss of the Nuzi samples. Their shapes included spheres, cones, tetrahedrons, disc, cylinders, and various odd shapes. I was able to add the third piece of the puzzle when, long after knowing of Pierre Amiet's work on the Susa bullae, I suddenly realized that my small "geometric objects" of the early Neolithic period were identical to the Susa abnati. It remained for me to prove that the recording system could be traced without discontinuity from 8500 to 3100 B.C. The three studies thus amounted to documenting the existence of a recording system based on abnati that was used in the five millennia that preceded writing and that continued well after the appearance of clay tablets.

The system of abnati seems to have been widespread in Mesopotamia. It was probably used in households to keep business accounts and to keep track of belongings, just as Iraqi shepherds today still keep count of their animals with pebbles.[13] It must have been used for all kinds of commodities, and the Bible pictures Yahweh keeping account of all humans with the same device: each living individual was represented by a token in a receptacle. Death was believed to occur when an angel would whirl a token away with a sling.[14]

What was the meaning of the various shapes of the abnati? We may presume, as mentioned by Amiet, that each shape represented a type of goods—garments, sheep, oil, etc. . . . and that the number of tokens of a kind, as well as their size, would confer the quantity. As I will discuss later, I also believe that some of the most common abnati had a numerical value and that the cone stood for one and the sphere for ten.

III. From a Recording to a Writing System

In excavations of sites from the IXth to the middle of the IVth millennium B.C., the abnati are usually found loose on the floor of the houses, courtyards, magazines, and in burials. Starting about 3100 B.C., some abnati are found enclosed in bullae.

---

[11] A. Leo Oppenheim "An Operational Device in Mesopotamian Bureaucracy," *Journal of Near Eastern Studies,* Vol. XVIII, 1958, pp. 121-28.

[12] Pierre Amiet. Glyptique susienne, mémoires de la délégation archéologique en Iran, Vol. XLIII, Paris, 1972.

[13] Thorkild Jacobsen. *In Human Origins,* Series II. Second Edition. University of Chicago Press, 1946, p. 245.

[14] Otto Eissfeldt. *Der Beutel der Lebendigen.* Berichte Über die Verhandlungen des Sachsischen Akademie der Wissenschaften zu Leipzig, Philologisch-Historische Klasse, Band 105, Heft 6, Akademie Verlag, Berlin, 1960.

Bullae are hollow clay balls that are found totally closed. When shaken they produce a rattling noise, indicating some loose content, and when broken they produce a certain number of abnati. During a period covering the second half of the IVth Mill and beginnings of the IIIrd Mill B.C., the bullae appear not only at Susa, where they were first identified, but also at various sites such as Chogha Mish,[15] Tepe Yahya,[16] and Shah-dad[17] in Iran; Warka[18] in Mesopotamia, and Habuba Kabira in Syria.[19] Bullae of the same appearance and covered with undeciphered signs have also been found at Abydos, in Egypt. However, they seem to be part of a funerary rite and their content and purpose seem totally different. One series of bullae found in a tomb contained small textile pellets.[20] In another case, the content was a tuft of child's hair.[21]

The bullae may have been devices to transfer abnati from one account to another in an institution, such as the Nuzi Palace mentioned above. The bullae were duly sealed for authentication, and Amiet notes that there are usually two different seal impressions,[22] probably one represents the accountant and the second the supervisor or recipient, such as a shepherd. Amiet suggested that the bullae may have also been used as as bill of lading, accompanying finished products, such as textiles manufactured in the country and transferred to the temple. The producer consigned his goods to the care of the middleman together with a bulla containing the number of tokens equivalent to the shipment.[23] In this case one seal would be from the sender and the second from the middleman. The recipient of the delivery could, by breaking the bulla, check the accuracy of the shipment upon arrival.

Accounting device, or bill of lading? – the interpretations are certainly not mutually exclusive. In general terms we may consider the bullae as convenient containers or envelopes to isolate the abnati representing a particular transaction. The bullae had, however, one great disadvantage: the opacity of clay did not allow any verification without breaking the bulla itself and with it the seals of authentification. To overcome this shortcoming, check marks began to be impressed on their surface repeating not only the number of abnati contained inside but also their shape (Ill. 4). One finds, for instance, a conical mark for a cone and a circular mark for a sphere. Of course, as soon as the system of check marks was generally adopted and understood, the abnati inside were no longer needed. The clay balls with abnati inside were replaced by a full clay ball—a tablet—with check marks on the outside. The marks on the clay bullae may therefore be viewed as the turning point between the archaic system of abnati and writing. Indeed, the check marks on the clay bullae are identical to the check marks on the clay tablets (Ill. 5). The first written signs made by the Sumerians—or their neighbors, the Elamites of Susa—were in fact representations of the shapes of abnati. As we know that the conical marks on the archaic tablets mean the number "1", we may assume that the small cone of the abnati system also had the value of "1". For the same reason the sphere probably meant "10".

[15]Helene J. Kantor, and Pinhas P. Delougaz, " New Light on the Emergence of Civilization in the Near East," *The Unesco Courier*, November, 1969, pp. 22-28.

[16]Denise Schmandt-Besserat and S. M. Alexander. *The First Civilization: the Legacy of Sumer*, Exhibit catalogue, pp. 52-53 No. 97.

[17]A. Hakemi, Catalogue de l'exposition: lut Xabis (Shahdad)–Premier symposium annuel de la recherche archeologique en Iran–Teheran, 1972. Pl. XXII. A.

[18]H. J. Lenzen. "New Discoveries at Warka in Southern Iraq," *Archaeology*, Vol. 17, No. 2, p. 128, 1964.

[19]Eva Stommenger. "Ausgrabungen in Habuba Kabira und Mumbaqat." *Archiv für Orientforschung*, 1973.

[20]T. Eric Peet. "A Remarkable Burial Custom of the Old Kingdom." *The Journal of Egyptian Archaeology*, Vol. III, 1916, p. 128.

[21]Winifred M. Crompton. "Two Clay Balls in the Manchester Museum." *The Journal of Egyptian Archaeology*, Vol. III, 1916, p. 128.

[22]Pierre Amiet. *Elam*, Auvers-sur-Oise, 1966, p. 70ff.

[23]Pierre Amiet. "Il y a 5000 ans les Elamites inventaient l'écriture," *Archeologia*, Vol. 12, 1966, pp. 16-23.

I am convinced that in the future we will be able to identify other abnati with a numerical connotation and in particular for the numbers 3, 5, and 3600. These numbers seem to be considered as entities in the Sumerian system of counting. Three, for instance, also meant "many," "much; 3600 was "everything"; and five was the root of the words for 6: *as*, five, a single one; 7: *imin*, five, two; 9: *ilimmu*, five, four.[24]

The impressed signs marked on the bullae could not reveal many details, and incised signs came to supplement them to render the more complicated abnati shapes on the tablets. Early pictographs may therefore reveal the meaning of some of the abnati representing commodities. The discs with one incised cross look similar to the sign for sheep; the abnu in the shape of a teardrop with an incision around the maximum diameter is identical to the sign for oil, and the cones with an incision around the base are the same as the sign for bread, etc. Viewed in this perspective, the abnati provide a meaningful explanation to the abstract shapes of the written signs that represented current commodities of daily life (Ill. 6). The abstraction process was elaborated well before writing, and five millennia of use of the abnati system contributed greatly to its development. The presence of true pictographs can further be explained by the introduction of new vocabulary that did not exist in the ancient system, such as chariot and sledge, or with commodities that were not usually traded, such as the ibex and the wild goat.

IV.   The Implications of the presence of the Abnati System at Khartoum and at Abydos

Although previously unsuspected, the presence of a recording system in Nubia dating back to 7000 B.C., does not seem implausible. Indeed most human societies at any level of culture have devised mnemonic systems to record facts of importance to them. The earliest known examples of the kind are the tallies carved in animal bones as early as 30,000 B.C. by the Paleolithic hunters of Europe. They have been interpreted by Marshack to be sophisticated calendars.[25] At the other extreme, the Peruvian Incas sent messages by means of threads or cords of different lengths, thicknesses, and colors called quipus.[26] Because of their simplicity, these mnemonic systems have survived in literate societies. This is the case of the Nuzi bulla in the IId Mill in Mesopotamia, and for the Romans who were using pebbles as calculi. Even today the abacus is widely used in Middle Eastern bazaars, and it is the necessary tool of all grade schoolers of Europe to learn how to count.

The puzzling thing is that this recording system of Khartoum is so similar to that used in the Middle East. It uses the same material, the same shapes, the same use of nicks and incisions for further notations: it seems in fact, to be one and the same. Scholars who have focused their attention on the study of Egyptian foreign relations, maintain that the pre-Gerzean cultures (3600 B.C.) drew their antecedents from Africa and were seemingly in almost complete isolation from the rest of the Middle East. The first rare tangible evidence of external relations with the East does not appear until the Badarian period (4000 B.C.) and consists of shells from the Red Sea, turquoise and copper from the Sinai, wood such as pine and precious woods such as cedar, cypress, and juniper from Syria.[27] It is also only at this time that isolated objects, which could be of foreign origin, such as pottery, begin to appear. The Khartoum abnati seem, therefore, to be the only link to the East three thousand years before the time of the first tenuous connections attested with the Middle East.

---

[24]Marvin A. Powell, Jr. "The Origin of the Sexagesimal System: The Interaction of Language and Writing," *Visible Language*, Vol. VI, No. 1, Winter 1972.

[25]A. Marschack. "The Roots of Civilization," McGraw-Hill, New York, 1972.

[26]D. Diringer. *Writing*, Thames and Hudson, London, 1962, Pl. 31-32.

[27]H. J. Kantor, "The Relative Chronology of Egypt and its Foreign Correlations before the Bronze Age" in R. S. Ehrich, *Chronologies in Old World Archaeology*, The University of Chicago Press, 1965.

It may be different if we keep in mind that, although objects of Eastern origin cannot be traced so far, currents of ideas can. In particular they include the practice of agriculture, animal and plant husbandry, and crafts such as pottery. Could the abanati be considered as part and parcel of the Neolithic package? The fact that they appear consistently in the earliest sedentary settlements throughout the entire Middle East, and that they are made of clay, which is the Neolithic material *par excellence,* would make me inclined to think so. The spread of what has been conveniently called "the Neolithic Revolution" was coming to Egypt from the East. This is, therefore, where we have to look for the possible origin of the Khartoum abnati. The closest geographic evidence for the presence of Abnati is in Palestine at the Natufian site of Ain Mallaha,[28] and abnati have also been found in the contemporary site of Tell Aswad in Syria.[29] There are no geographical boundaries between Egypt, Palestine, and Syria. The Sinai Peninsula has water holes regularly spaced along the Mediterranean coast, and it would be difficult to imagine this land bridge without a perennial movement of people, in particular pastoralists, who followed the rhythm of the rainy seasons or were pushed by droughts. The movements of ideas, which spread through the Middle East crossing deserts, mountain ranges and seas, may thus explain the presence of abnati in distant places such as Khartoum.

The abnati of Abydos appear on a totally different background. A great deal of evidence exists of Egypt's extensive relations with Mesopotamia and Elam during the Gerzean period, *ca.* 3500 B.C. Contacts took place either by the overland route through Palestine and Syria that began at headwaters of the Euphrates, or by sea around the Arabian peninsula and up the Red Sea. The evidence of these contacts consists of objects, such as cylinder seals, and stylistic motifs, such as the line of animals, the tree of life, composite creatures, and the master of animals. Around 3000 B.C., while the relations with Syria seem to have intensified. This is illustrated by the great number of Syro-Palestinian pottery vessels, which probably contained oil and perfume, found in royal and private tombs.[30]

The presence of an early recording system shared by the early Neolithic cultures of Egypt and the rest of the Middle East in the IXth and IIIrd Mill B.C. was totally unsuspected and raises important questions. Can we, for instance, assume that the same shapes of abnati had different meanings in different places, or should we consider the archaic recording system as a *lingua franca* throughout the Middle East? One argument in favor of the latter is the fact that the meaning of the cone for "1" and for the sphere for "10" seem to have been shared by a wide area, including at least Mesopotamia and Elam because the two retained this value in both the Sumerian and Elamite script. Of course each shape of abnati could be expressed orally in different languages without alteration of the meaning since the tokens did not stand for specific sounds. A second argument is that a basic similarity exists between the early scripts of Sumer, Elam, Egypt and the Indus Valley. Will the abnati system prove to be the common ancestor hypothesized by Diringer for the four early Middle Eastern writing systems? [31]

V.   Conclusion

The abnati were a recording system that preceded writing by 5,000 years. The early counters were shaped from clay in varied geometric and odd shapes and probably represented numbers or items to be recorded. About the IVth millennium B.C., it was customary to enclose the specific number of a transaction in a clay envelope (called a "bulla"). For convenience, the number and shapes of the counters enclosed were repeated on the surface of the bulla by means of punched marks of the same shape and number. The marks, were, in fact, the

---

[28]Personal Communication of Jean Perrot.

[29]Henri de Contenson. "Tell Aswad, Fouilles de 1971," *Annales Archéologiques Arabes Syriennes,* 1972.

[30]H. J. Kantor, *op. cit.,* 1965.

[31]D. Diringer. *op. cit.,* 1962, p. 36.

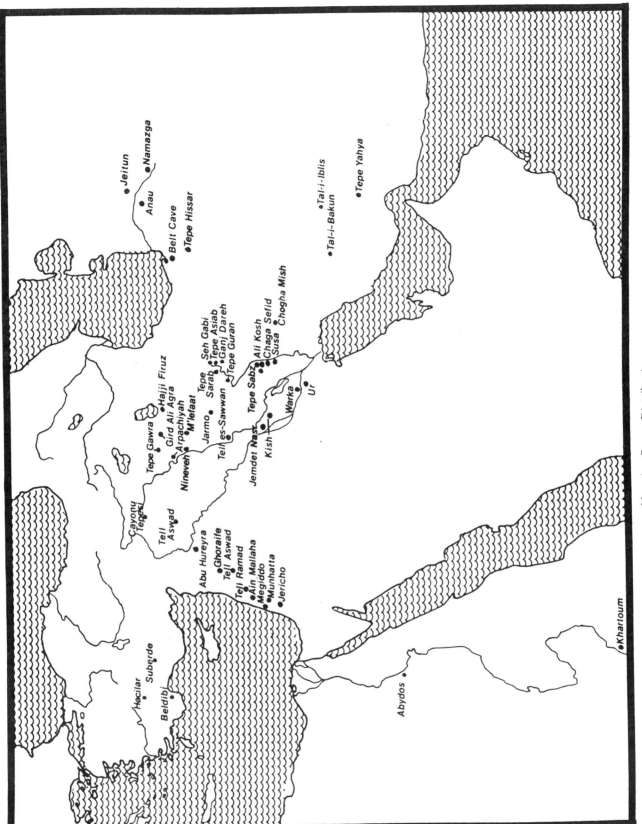

Map 1. Space Distribution.

earliest pictographs that developed and evolved on the Sumerian and Elamite tablets. These facts imply that writing was not a sudden discovery brought about by the Sumerians or Elamites but the continuum of an indigenous recording system shared by many cultures of the Middle East. The most impressive feature of this early three-dimensional system may not be its antiquity (which pushed back the origin of writing by five millennia) but rather its wide extent (Map 1). The recent discovery of geometric objects in Egypt indicate that it may have shared a prewriting system of recording with the other cultures of the ancient Middle East. It may explain some of the similarities of the four early Middle Eastern systems of writing: Sumerian, proto-Elamite, Egyptian and that from the Indus Valley.

*Perspectives on Irrigation Civilization
in Pharaonic Egypt*

by

Karl W. Butzer
The University of Chicago

Irrigation agriculture provided the economic base for the first civilizations in the Near East. Most alluvial soils in subtropical and tropical environments are naturally fertile and agriculturally productive where water is adequate. The added element of labor and technology—implied in the concept of irrigation—optimizes the distribution of available water to improve median crop yields and to reduce their annual variablility. The potential yields of such an intensive form of land use greatly increase carrying capacity and may allow human populations to remain closer to such carrying capacities. Given the primitive communication systems inherent to early civilizations, a ring of high-productivity lands could support large populations within reasonable distance of high-order central places. It is therefore not surprising that the archeological and historical records suggest a more than casual coincidence between foci of irrigation farming, urban centers, and evidence for complex economic and social stratification.

The apparent relationships between irrigation farming and socio-political forms has long intrigued historians of one generation, and social scientists of another. One classic view was articulated by V. Gordon Childe (1929, and later), who argued that irrigation provided the agricultural surplus essential to economically-complex societies, thereby creating opportunity for the development of vertically-structured, urban civilizations. Another, related hypothesis was explicated by Karl Wittfogel (1938, and later), who linked "hydraulic" civilizations with his socio-political model of a highly-organized peasantry, exploited by an absolute, bureaucratic, and centralized state ("oriental despotism"). These notions have provoked the growth of a prodigious body of secondary, discoursive literature as well as several fresh archeological or historical analyses at various scales. Yet, the ecological framework of an ancient hydraulic society has never been systematically examined. Any ecological perspectives to emerge in these general discussions have considered too few variables or have been patently erroneous, and their significance has accordingly been dismissed or ignored.

This is unfortunate, since the basic "procedures" of a cultural ecology were outlined over two decades ago by Steward (1954). Their basic intent has become central to much of the best archeological theory, but their implementation has proved elusive, in the main part because the data base is or appears to be inadequate. I have long suspected that the comparative lack of success in implementing a more effective ecological approach in past contexts has been symptomatic of disciplinary isolation and ineffectual methodologies. An ecological framework should focus on three independent variables, on or through which the fourth variable is modelled. These independent variables are environment, technology, and population (including settlement and demography). The dependent variable in this equation is social organization and differentiation. Interrelationships between nature and culture cannot be deciphered without a sophisticated comprehension of the environment, nor without reasonably good information on technology and population. Such relationships are rarely appreciated by the many social scientists who concern themselves exclusively with the dependent variable of the above equation.

The emergence and evolution of an hydraulic civilization in the Nile Valley provide a unique possibility to explore this critical matter of cultural ecology. It is quite pertinent to Childe and Wittfogel, and to what has been written and argued since. Here there is an unusual wealth of cultural and environmental data that span five millennia of historical time and an even longer range of prehistory. My own interests in the natural and cultural landscape complex of Egypt have profited from repeated research efforts on Egypt, interrupted by extended studies in Spain, Ethiopia, and South Africa dealing with both similar and different time periods. Each time I returned to the Egyptian materials with more experience and broader perspectives. The result has been a systematic attempt to analyze the archeological and historical record of environment, technology, settlement, and land use in ancient Egypt. The data are at once imperfect and exciting, and are more fully documented in the original publication (Butzer 1976). The present paper outlines the basic arguments and re-examines some existing hypotheses.

The Nile floodplain and delta represent free-draining, seasonally-inundated alluvial surfaces. In such a model, exemplified by the Nile or the Mississippi, the river generally remains within its channel but, in the case of the Nile, between late summer and early autumn, it spills out to flood the low-lying basins to an average depth of 1.5 m, laying down a thin increment of fertile silt and clay before the waters drain back naturally into the river, or evaporate from the floodplain. The highest alluvial ground follows the river channel, or that of its major branches, in the form of silt berms or natural levees that are topped by flood waters only briefly during 1-in-10-year episodes of peak discharge. The flood basins are subdivided by such levees, and further demarcated by the rapid rise of land at the desert margins. Such natural basins vary in size from a few square kilometers to over a hundred, being largest where the alluvial valley is widest and where the river is farthest away from one desert edge. The flood waters enter by low points in the levees, often along small but defined diverging channels, to drain back into the Nile, as the floods recede, by a network of gathering streams. Flood stage comes earliest in the south, latest in the north, with the flood basins filling for an average of 4 to 6 weeks, and then draining except for small, residual water bodies or marsh in the low-lying backswamps.

The hydrology of the Nile River is remarkably predictable by the standards of other river systems. The upper basin taps two major climatic provinces for its water: the summer monsoon in Ethiopia and the southern Sudan, and the double, equinoctial rainy season of Uganda and Tanzania. The blending of these water supplies south of the axis of the Sahara, and the specific hydrographic pattern of river basins at different latitudes, provides a comparatively balanced and reliable flood regime between August and November, followed by a long low-water season in which the river is increasingly sluggish, but essentially never fails. The basic seasons can be easily recognized according to the state of the river—its minute fluctuations of level and persistent trends, its color and condition. The temporal framework thus provided is far more explicit and foolproof than any available elsewhere on the basis of hydrographic or climatic seasons, and would have been recognized long before the invention of an astronomical calendar.

Given these physical premises, which have persisted with little change since at least 25,000 years ago, the biota of the Nile flood-plain received a new lease on life each year as the waters began to rise. Such a hydrological system, combined with the specific topographic arrangement within a "convex" floodplain, provided a natural mechanism of irrigation and drainage. Along other, comparable African rivers it supports a fringing forest on the banks and levees, a grassy savanna on the floors of the flood basins, and sedge, reed and papyrus marsh or lotus-studded ponds in the backswamps, channel cut-offs, and in coastal proximity. The levees provide suitable settlement sites, while the basin floors can be cultivated as the flood waters recede, or generally used for grazing until the next flood. The excellent record of Upper Paleolithic and Epi-Paleolithic settlement shows a decided preference for riverbank sites and there was no conceivable need to "colonize" the alluvial lands at a comparatively late date, by first draining the flood basins and clearing any hypothetical jungle-like thickets.

It has, then, been widely overlooked that the Nile flood basins are free-draining and naturally irrigated. Upper Paleolithic groups harvested a variety of plant foods and successfully hunted a broad spectrum of aquatic, woodland, savanna, and desert game from encampments located on the river banks. Equally so, Neolithic groups since about 5000 B.C. grazed their herds quite freely and, as the floods receded, planted fields for a single crop that grew to maturity on the basis of stored soil moisture and a relatively high groundwater table. Even in late Pleistocene times, rainfall in Egypt proper would have been inadequate for agriculture away from the waters of the Nile. But natural irrigation was always available, so that *artificial* irrigation was supplementary rather than essential for agricultural subsistence on the floodplain. The purpose of artificial irrigation in the Nile Valley was to increase crop acreage and to help equalize year-to-year productivity versus relatively small but ecologically significant fluctuations in flood level and persistance.

The technology and organization of Egyptian irrigation in Pharaonic times was consequently geared to a specific environmental system and intended to extend and intensify the agricultural base. This was implemented in the form of traditional basin irrigation, such as persisted in Upper Egypt until late in the 19th century A.D. Modern analogs suggest several logical steps for rudimentary, artificial irrigation. Deliberate flooding and draining of natural basins, by breaches or more elaborate sluice gates in the natural levees, is the first and most obvious procedure. Such controlled irrigation would be easiest in the smaller flood basins of southern Egypt and, further north, primarily along the narrow alluvial strip east of the river. Eventually, the natural levees would be strengthened and equalized by superimposition of longitudinal dikes. Ultimately the larger flood basins would be subdivided into more manageable units by transverse dikes. Development of such an irrigation system, particularly in the larger basins, required a massive input of labor and large-scale community cooperation much like it did a century ago. This applied both to the regular opening and closing of the dikes, particularly at times of exceptionally high floods, as well as to the initial construction and maintenance of artificial dikes. Canals, except for ditches, cut through dikes, were probably unknown at first, but by Ist Dynasty times (ca. 3050 B.C.) networks of small canals served to distribute water to the fields below sluice gates. However, large-scale canalization was only implemented in Egypt during the 19th century A.D. Lift irrigation, other than manually—by single bucket or by a shoulder-yoke to support two buckets—was not practiced until the later 18th Dynasty (ca. 1400 B.C.), when the lever or shaduf was introduced. The far more effective waterwheel or saqiya diffused through Egypt much later, during the last 3 centuries B.C. In effect, lift irrigation was only utilized on a localized, horticultural basis in Pharaonic Egypt, serving to water vegetable, fruit, and ornamental gardens. Summer garden crops, or cultivation of the higher-lying levees, were impossible without lift irrigation, and even in Ptolemaic times, when summer staples such as sorghum were introduced, the limitations of natural fertility precluded more than one crop per year on any one plot of land.

The prevalent image of intensive and sophisticated irrigation in Pharaonic Egypt is, then, misleading. During the early Middle Kingdom, ca. 2000 B.C., it appears that pasture and cultivation were practiced on roughly equal areas of the Nile floodplain, while a millennium earlier it is probable that hunting was still important in extensive areas of unutilized "wilderness."

To what extent was this progressive development of Egypt centrally directed or organized? The mace-head of the Scorpion King, ca. 3100 B.C., shows Pharaoh ceremonially breaching a dike, to inaugurate the flood season—as interpreted in analogy to early 19th century custom. There are a number of 6th Dynasty allusions to the cutting of canals by the king, but large-scale development is first suggested for the 12th Dynasty (1991-1786 B.C.), which "opened up" the Faiyum Depression, a low-lying marshy adjunct to the Nile Valley with a central lake. Expansion of the cultivated lands into the northern half of the Nile Delta was apparently favored by the Ramessids (1320-1070 B.C.), the Saite Dynasty (663-525 B.C.), and particularly by the Ptolemies (323-30 B.C.), who also organized a systematic expansion of cultivation in the Faiyum, constructing a radial irrigation network similar to those prevalent in ancient Mesopotamia.

Unlike the entrepreneurial and mercantile administration of the Ptolemies, the agricultural policies of the Egyptian Pharaohs seem to have been mainly directed towards administration of the scattered royal domains and the rewarding of retainers, veterans, and temples with land grants. This did lead to demonstrable founding of new settlements or to the intensification of productivity in the Delta and Faiyum, and to some degree in more thinly-settled areas upvalley. But there never was a centrally-organized irrigation system, nor a formal bureaucracy to deal with irrigation. In fact, water legislation is conspicuously absent among the written records relevant to the Nile Valley (as opposed to the Libyan Desert oases and Syria), indicating that irrigation procedure and water rights were already firmly committed to oral tradition in late prehistoric times, requiring no subsequent redefinition. Despite the symbolic identificaiton of Pharaoh with the annual flood cycle from the earliest times, irrigation was implemented at the community level, by the input of all able-bodied men, just as it was in the 19th century A.D. Each natural flood basin formed a logical unit of social organization, for general maintenance and effective interdigitation of the artificial subbasins. As the settlement record shows, such basins were commonly linked to central places positioned at intervals along the length of the Nile or its major branches. Several larger and a number of smaller basins of this type constituted the basic polities, or nomes, of Egypt. The political infrastructure was therefore anchored—however indirectly—within an ecological framework and with reference to scale components of the fundamental social organization. In contrast to radial systems, where water inputs are artificially regulated at each distributional node, there was no competition for water between individual flood basins, each of which had direct access to the Nile and was unaffected by water use or regulation upstream.

The distribution of settlements in Pharaonic Egypt provides clear evidence of population gradients and centers of concentration. Densities were markedly greater in the narrower floodplain segments in the south, and in the far north, near Memphis. It can be argued that intensive utilization of the intervening section of broader floodplain was rendered difficult by the great size of the natural flood basins. These would have required massive labor to bring under control, and there is evidence for a persistence of extensive as opposed to intensive land use in these underdeveloped nomes until at least the 12th century B.C. It is also possible that internal colonization was inhibited by a nome structure originally based on tribal subdivisions among the Nile flood basins. Only in the New Kingdom did government resettlement of veterans and mercenaries, and more spontaneous emigration from the densely populated, smaller, southern nomes, begin to fill out the broad floodplain north of Abydos. But even this process was only completed in Coptic times some two millennia later. This illustrates that population gradients need not be population pressures, and that Carneiro's (1972) ideas on the matter represent a far from universal model.

Given the local organization and rudimentary technology of Pharaonic irrigation, it is probable that periodically deficient or excessive floods kept population levels well below carrying capacity, particularly during times of incompetent government. So, for example, the poor flood of A.D. 1877 was only 2 m. below average, but it left as much as 75% of the land of some provinces unirrigated and therefore uncultivable. Similarly, excessively high floods, such as in A.D. 1818-19, breached transverse dikes, razed settlements, destroyed food stores and seed stocks, and decimated livestock. Control over such natural catastrophes was technologically impossible in Pharaonic Egypt. And, at the administrative level there is no evidence for centrally-organized food storage and redistribution until the mid-18th Dynasty (ca. 1450 B.C.), when the local temples assumed redistributory and managerial functions that could potentially serve to alleviate the impact of periodically poor crop yields. Expansion of populations to levels somewhat closer to carrying capacity should therefore have been increasingly possible during times of effective government. Conversely, the negative demographic impacts of recurrent intervals of economic decline would have been accentuated.

The available information on fluctuations of the Nile floods indicates a general downward trend during the third millennium from the 1st Dynasty to the end of the Old Kingdom, with one or more sets of catastrophic Nile failures between perhaps 2250 and 1950 B.C.; flood levels generally improved thereafter, with at least 28 exceptionally high floods of disastrous proportions ca. 1840-1770 B.C. (see Bell, 1970, 1971, 1975). Floods remained generally high until about 1200 B.C., after which they declined rapidly and then remained lower until at least the time of Herodotus. These trends are closely comparable to those documented by radiocarbon-dated lake-level or flood-discharge fluctuations in the central Sudan, in Ethiopia and the Kenya Rift, as well as in the Chad Basin and southern Sahara. When calibrated to calendar years they can be dated more precisely: critical reductions of lake levels and stream discharge began 2700 ± 100 B.C., were reversed in the wake of substantially wetter conditions in subsaharan Africa 1850 ± 50 B.C., with another negative hydrological trend beginning 1200 ± 50 B.C.

In the Nile Valley, there was a 30% decline in discharge during the course of the Old Kingdom, a trend that would have favored greater reliance on artificial irrigation. It is also difficult not to see causal linkages between the disastrous economic recession or the collapse of the political order after the death of Pepi II (ca. 2260 B.C.) and the Egyptian "lamentations" describing Nile failures, desiccation of marshlands, severe famine, general poverty, and mass deaths. During the second half of the Middle Kingdom (2040-1715 B.C.), a new form of stress was created by the Nile: one flood out of three or four equalled or exceeded the highest floods of the 19th century A.D.. It remains to be explored whether the agricultural system was able to withstand such a battering, and whether the collapse of the Middle Kingdom and the successful infiltration of the Asiatic Hyksos were preconditioned by Nile-related economic deterioration. For the late Ramessid period there is significant evidence that food prices—with respect to metals—were rapidly inflated ca. 1170-1100 B.C., most likely in response to inadequate harvests and low Nile floods. The significance of the inferred ecological stress for the abrupt decline of Egypt during the 12th century B.C. may have been considerable.

These examples have not yet been proven beyond reasonable doubt, but they serve to suggest that major segments of ancient Egyptian history may be unintelligible without recourse to an ecological perspective. They further suggest that the cyclic crises in hydraulic civilizations that Wittfogel (1938) attributed to social disequilibrium, in response to overexploitation of the masses by an unproductive ruling bureaucracy, may in fact have rather different explanations, such as the recurrence interval and magnitude of natural catastrophes.

A multi-tiered economy was already established in Egypt by 3000 B.C., judging by the monumental architecture of the 1st Dynasty, while complex social stratification in the urban sector is abundantly evident from the written records of the Old Kingdom. Yet the Mesopotamian model of rapid population growth leading to greater competition for water, increased labor efficiency, intensified irrigation, a more intricate division of labor, social stratification and, ultimately, state superstructures (Adams 1972), cannot be documented for Egypt. Competition for water was never an issue, except locally. At the social and administrative level, flood control and irrigation were also managed locally, and well into the 19th century A.D. most Egyptians continued to live the traditional way of life in villages and small centers where division of labor and class distinctions remained minimal, in a subsistence enomomy based on irrigation. Although Old Kingdom Egypt (ca. 2850-2250 B.C.) was strongly centralized in terms of its political superstructure, there is reason to assume that the infrastructure, at least in Upper Egypt, continued to function on more traditional lines via a number of indirect agents and agencies that mediated between the capital and the local communities. Ecological problems appear to have been preeminently handled at the local level, so that the development of a professional, full-time bureaucracy must be related to a different social impetus. There is, then, no direct causal relationship between hydraulic agriculture and the development of Pharaonic political structure and society.

Hydraulic agriculture did indeed provide the indispensable economic resource base for the complex, state-centered society that emerged in the form of the Old Kingdom, but high economic productivity is essential to any complex society. More relevant to the socio-political system of Pharaonic Egypt is the socio-economic anchoring of the nomes into the explicit ecological framework of a riverine oasis. These primeval nomes appear to have provided the necessary political infrastructure that allowed the military unification of Egypt. Similarly, there is growing evidence that the economic history of ancient Egypt was primarily one of continuous ecological readjustment to a variable water supply, combined with repeated efforts to intensify or expand land use in order to increase productivity. It is in this sense that hydraulic civilization in Egypt remains inconceivable without its ecological determinants, but not by a linear causality model of stress favoring irrigation development, so creating a managerial bureaucracy, and ultimately leading to despotic control.

The Egyptian case study outlined here appears to have implications for other, early hydraulic civilizations. There is good reason to believe that sociological hypotheses are by themselves inadequate to explicate the processes involved in the emergence of floodplain civilizations. Indeed, it would appear that the origins of early irrigation civilizations are far more complex than existing assumptions and paradigms allow. It therefore becomes pertinent to reexamine other critical areas from an ecological perspective.

ACKNOWLEDGEMENT

The research underlying this essay was possible only with
the benefit of repeated discussions with Klaus Baer (Chicago).

References

ADAMS, R. M.
  1972   "Demography and the 'Urban Revolution' in Lowland Mesopotamia." In *Population Growth: Anthropological Implications,* ed. B. Spooner, pp. 60-63. Cambridge: M.I.T. Press.
BELL, BARBARA
  1970   "The Oldest Records of the Nile Floods." *Geographical Journal* 136:569-73.
  1971   "The Dark Ages in Ancient History: I. The First Dark Age in Egypt." *American Journal of Archaeology* 75:1-26.
  1975   "Climate and the History of Egypt: The Middle Kingdom." *American Journal of Archaeology* 79:223-69.
BUTZER, K. W.
  1976   *Early Hydraulic Civilization in Egypt: A Study in Cultural Ecology.* Chicago: University of Chicago Press.
CARNEIRO, R. L.
  1972   "From Autonomous Villages to the State: A Numerical Estimation." In *Population Growth: Anthropological Implications,* ed. B. Spooner, pp. 64-77. Cambridge: M.I.T. Press.
CHILDE, V. G.
  1929   *The Most Ancient East.* London: Routledge and Kegan Paul.
STEWARD, J. H.
  1954   "The Concept and Method of Cultural Ecology." In *Theory of Culture Change*, pp. 30-42. Urbana: University of Illinois.
WITTFOGEL, K. A.
  1938   "Die Theorie der orientalischen Gesellschaft." *Zeitschrift für Sozialforschung* 7:90-122.

Aspects of Egyptian Art: Function and Aesthetic[1]

by

William Kelly Simpson
Yale University
Museum of Fine Arts, Boston

Our appreciation of the art of Ancient Egypt is enhanced through an understanding of its development through three thousand years of permanence and change. As with the arts of Africa, Pre-Columbian America, and many other parts of the world, we must first recognize that Egyptian art can only be understood as an integral aspect of Egyptian religion. This does not necessarily mean that we must have a comprehensive understanding of Egyptian religion in order to understand its art, but that we cannot disassociate a statue or wall relief from its original use.

Statues and wall scenes were in fact completely functional and even utilitarian, in the same sense as a cooking pot, an agricultural implement, or a vehicle is utilitarian. A statue served a purpose as clearly as did a shovel or hoe, although the purpose in the former case may have been magical. "As a substantial part of Egyptian art was never intended to be seen by mortal eyes, the manifestation of decorative and aesthetic qualities cannot have been its principal aim, which was undoubtedly of a metaphysical and magical nature. . . Sculptural representations were consequently not primarily things of beauty and delectation, but magical entities fraught with fateful significance."[2]

It is equally clear that the function of a statue is not as immediately evident as the function of a hoe or an axe. What then, in simplest terms, were some of the uses for which statues were created? As might be expected, these uses were multiple as well as specific.

The tomb statues of the deceased which were placed in the offering chambers of the burials of the Old Kingdom served as representatives or deputies of the departed individual. These had the purpose of receiving the offerings of food, drink, clothing, and other produce and consumer goods which were brought to the chapel under contractual agreements with his survivors and suppliers. Copies of such legal documents have occasionally been found. The statue served as a substitute for the deceased for the purpose of receiving these goods and hearing the spells recited at prescribed intervals by the scroll-reading priests, and as the intermediary whereby the mouth, eyes, and ears of the deceased could be magically opened and rendered functional by the spells read by the priests.

The temple statues, on the other hand, represented the individual as a participant in the temple processions and ritual feasts. The individual continued, therefore, even after his death, as an active participant on the

---

[1] A substantial part of the text of this lecture has been utilized in two recent publications by the author: *The Face of Egypt: Permanence and Change in Egyptian Art.* The Katonah Gallery, Katonah, New York, 1977, and *The Offering Chapel of Sekhem-ankh-ptah in the Museum of Fine Arts, Boston.* Department of Egyptian and Ancient Near Eastern Art, Museum of Fine Arts, Boston, 1976.

[2] Erik Iversen, *Canon and Proportions in Egyptian Art*, 2nd ed., Aris and Phillips, Warminster, England, 1975, 6.

feast days in the presence of his gods and as a consumer of the income of property donated to the temple by him.[3] For proper acknowledgement of the receipt of this income, whether in tomb chapel or temple, it was essential to have the name and official position of the individual inscribed on the statue or relief.

In brief, the statues of officials were fashioned to serve as a kind of insurance that the man, even after death, would continue to enjoy the consumer goods to which he was entitled by prior contractual arrangement and to participate in the temple festivals. From the form of the statue, the position of the hands, and the nature of the inscription, it is often possible to determine whether the statue was fashioned for tomb or for temple, although types created for one of these functions were often borrowed for the other.

A third type of statue is the *ex voto,* or statue offered to fulfill a vow. These statues are of gods and goddesses and their worshippers, and were placed as an act of donation in the temples. To this category belong the many bronzes of the Third Intermediate Period and of the later Saite and Ptolemaic Periods. Many of them have the name and offices of the donor inscribed on the base to insure proper recognition of the act of piety. Often these bronzes were part of elaborate compositions relating to the barques of the gods.[4]

The three types cited above apply to statues and statuettes of the nobles and bureaucrats represented in Egyptian texts. The situation was similar for the king, but not identical. In the major temples the statues of the king, sometimes with his queen and sons and daughters, were set up on a monumental scale in an imposing architectural setting provided by the pillars and columns. These statues had the additional function of serving to impress the viewer with the might and piety of the ruler.

Egyptian art, as well as much of Egyptian literature,[5] was very much in the service of the propaganda of the state and the state religion and corresponds to the modern media of public relations and advertising. Exhibited on the walls of the temples was the figure of the king smiting the enemies of Egypt and conquering foreign peoples, as well as engaging in a series of pious rituals in the presence of the gods. Detailed lists of donations to the temples, both from agricultural estates and from the spoils of war, were inscribed on the walls as a permanent record of the ruler's devotion. In return for these donations the ruler expected to receive on a contractual basis a long and successful life on earth and life among the gods after death. The prosperity of the land of Egypt with the annual inundation of the Nile, the abundance of the crops, and the increase of the herds of cattle depended upon the good will and favor of the gods. It was the duty of the king to satisfy the gods through offerings and service and, as it were, to bribe them to insure a good harvest at home, the successful exploitation of mineral wealth, and security of the country's borders. The king is thereby shown as the player of a role. He enacts the rituals, presents the offerings before the gods, and conquers the traditional enemies of the land in exchange for the gods' approval and guarantee of the prosperity and security of Egypt.[6]

The viewer of today judges the merits of a statue or relief on its aesthetic value rather than in terms of the success of its magical function. This must also have been the case in Ancient Egypt among competing craftsmen and their clients, and on occasion the work of the past was studied and even copied in detail.

---

[3]H. Bonnet, "Herkunft und Bedeutung der naophoren Statue," *Mitteilungen des Deutschen Archäologischen Instituts Abteilung Kairo* 17 (1961) 91-98.

[4]E. L. B. Terrace, "Three Egyptian Bronzes," *Bulletin of the Museum of Fine Arts, Boston* 57 (1959) 48-53.

[5]Georges Posener, *Littérature et politique dans l'Égypte de la XIIe dynastie,* Bibliothèque de l'École des hautes études, Fasc. 307, Honoré Champion, Paris, 1956.

[6]Erik Hornung, *Geschichte als Fest,* Wissenschaftliche Buchgesellschaft, Darmstadt, 1966.

From Dynasty 26 there are examples of close copies of wall reliefs and paintings of the Middle Kingdom and the New Kingdom.[7] At about the same time reliefs of these earlier periods were overlaid with red grid lines by the copyists.[8]

It has often been noted that the typical Egyptian statue retains the austerity of the rectangular block or cube from which it was carved. The Museum of Fine Arts in Boston has a series of unfinished small statuettes of King Mycerinus of Dynasty 4 which exhibit various stages of completion.[9] After the initial cutting of the block, a grid of red lines was overlaid on it as a guide. These aided the sculptor and represented the prescribed canonical points, such as, the top of the brow, the chin, the knees, and the feet. Traces of these grids can be seen in the statues just cited.

It is evident that statues were intended to be seen from the front and the sides, rarely in a three-quarter view, and seldom from the back. Indeed, the placement of many statues against the pillars and walls which served as their architectural setting prevented the viewer from seeing the back. Often the back consists of a sort of wall in one piece with the statue, or a pillar, or an extension of the seat.

In general, the individual's name and offices or the name of the reigning king were inscribed on the base, the sides of the seat, the space between two figures, the back support, part of the garment, the front of the cloak, or any other convenient space. When no inscription is present, we must assume one of several possible reasons: the setting or emplacement made the inscription unnecessary; the statue was carved by a sculptor for a client still unspecified; the text was in ink and is now effaced; or the part of the statue with the text is missing. Since the statue served as the representative of the individual, it was more important for it to have the credentials of an inscribed name than for it to resemble facially and physically the specific individual for whom it was created.

It is interesting to assess the ways in which the Egyptian artist dealt with the subject of portraiture and the extent to which the statue or relief reflects the traits of the subject. In the case of the kings and also some of the great officials there are numerous representations of the same person. In general, Egyptian art reflects the particular shape and features of the individual, and it is often possible to assign a head which lacks an identifying text to a specific king or more rarely to a courtier.[10] The statue of the official Hemiun of Dynasty 4 in the Hildesheim Museum can be compared to a relief portrait from his tomb in the Boston Museum, and a funerary head of a treasury official named Nofer of the same period in the Boston Museum resembles the reliefs from the official's chapel. However, there is also a general tendency within a dynasty or reign for a certain sameness in portraiture, influenced to some degree by the official likeness of the king. This attempt to represent a standardized ideal is obviously at variance with the appearance of a particular individual. The faces of a husband and wife in a pair statue, for example, may seem identical. In such cases, the artist expressed a standardized ideal rather than an adherence to fact. In addition, there are examples of sculptures which were turned out in large numbers for sale to clients, carved by a sculptor who probably had no specific individual in mind as he worked.

The head is usually the only part really individualized even in the best work. The iconography of the body, however well executed, merely makes a statement: a prosperous fatness to indicate wealth and well-

---

[7]Portions of the tomb of Aba at Thebes, an official of the reign of Psamtik I of Dynasty 26, were copied from the tomb of an earlier namesake at Deir el Gebrawi of Dynasty 6: N. de G. Davies, *The Rock Tombs of Deir el Gebrâwi,* Part I. *Tomb of Aba and Smaller Tombs of the Southern Group,* Archaeological Survey of Egypt, Eleventh Memoir, London, 1902.

[8]Iversen, *Canon and Proportions.*

[9]George A. Reisner, Mycerinus: The Temples of the Third Pyramid at Giza, Harvard University Press, Cambridge, 1931, pls. 62-63.

[10]Claude Vandersleyen, "Objectivité des portraits égyptiens," *Bulletin de la Société française d'Egyptologie* 73 (1975) 5-27.

being, a trim athletic build to indicate confidence and vitality, or signs of age to indicate maturity or wisdom. These features connote well-being, vitality, or wisdom instead of a realistic rendering of the subject. Portraits of Akhenaten and Nefertiti executed during the course of their reign seem to show an increasingly younger couple, contrary to reality.[11] Throughout the history of art, and even today, there is a tendency to stress youthfulness at some times and maturity at other times.

These tendencies underline a significant feature of Egyptian art: a commitment to representing and explaining things as they should be or must be ideally, as opposed to the impressions of a fleeting moment or the recording of emotions. Serenity and seriousness of purpose characterize the faces, and one looks in vain for traces of laughter or agony. In carved relief and in tomb painting there is a certain amount of characterization: the wailing and distraught professional mourners following the funeral procession, the gnarled herdsman, the joyful dancers, the famine-stricken enemies, the outlandish physiognomy, physique and costume of foreigners, and even the suffering of wounded animals in the hunting scenes. Yet in all these cases the emphasis is on the explicative gestures of the figures rather than on facial features and emotions.

To describe some of the differences in the Egyptian method or representation, recent scholars have used two contrasting terms, perspective and aspective.[12] In perspective drawing the nearer figures are larger and those in the distance correspondingly smaller. This method was alien to most of Egyptian art. Aspective art emphasizes the qualities of an object or group of objects from the viewpoint of their geometrical form and their importance in a hierarchical order. The most important figures are shown on a much larger scale, irrespective of their placement in the composition. Most figures are placed on ground lines and arranged in bands one above the other. In the representation of a box, a draftsman may show the front, top, and both sides, although the eye cannot see all four of these elements at the same time. In representing the saddle bag on a donkey, the side not seen by the viewer may be flipped up to stress its existence.

Our understanding of Egyptian art is enhanced when we restrict our inquiry to a specific period, medium, and function. Such a case is the relief of the offering chapels of the Old Kingdom (ca. 2700-2200 B.C.). The numerous structures of the officials at the great Memphite cemeteries at Giza, Sakkara, Abusir, and elsewhere have long been known as mastaba tombs on the analogy of their shape to the common bench seen in the villages to this day (Arabic: *mastaba*).[13] These structures comprise two essential elements: a subterranean burial chamber in the rock, with the coffin of the deceased and associated burial gifts and equipment, and a massive superstructure, in stone or brick, usually with an offering chapel, above ground. The superstructure exhibits a wide variation in its arrangements and frequently has interior and exterior offering chambers as well as one or more statue chambers (serdabs). The offering chamber was an area open to the living where the cult of the deceased was celebrated, food offerings delivered, and spells recited for his benefit in the hereafter. The burial chamber, reached through a shaft in the mass of the superstructure, was intended to be sealed off forever.

The offering chamber was frequently decorated in bas-relief with a series of standard funerary formulae and prescribed scenes from a wide repertory. The essential scene is that of the owner seated before a table of offering breads partaking of his meal, for the principal context of the entire program is the provision of sustenance for the owner in the hereafter. This concept is expanded and amplified, particularly in the later mastabas of Dynasties 5 and 6, with a host of scenes of daily life on the estate. The owner views them passively from the vantage point of a departed spirit. In addition to the texts which provide his

---

[11]Cyril Aldred, *Akhenaten, Pharaoh of Egypt: A New Study*, Thames and Hudson, London, 1968.

[12]Emma Brunner-Traut, "Epilogue - Aspective," in Heinrich Schäfer, *Principles of Egyptian Art*, ed. with an epilogue by Emma Brunner-Traut, translated and edited, with an introduction, by John Baines. Clarendon Press, Oxford, 1974.

[13]Auguste Mariette, *Les mastabas de l'ancien empire*, F. Vieweg, Paris, 1884-1885, pp. 22-23.

name and the offices which he had held on earth, there are captions and identifications to these scenes of daily life, as well as the standard ritual formulae. Foremost among the latter is the invocation-of-the-offering text, beginning with the statement that it is the king and the gods who have accorded him a burial in the west and granted him the rights and privileges specified.[14] Provision is made for the upkeep of the chapel through the entailment of the produce of specified properties, usually from agricultural holdings, and through the employment of officials and custodians, who were paid from the income of these properties to conduct the services in the chapel, deliver the meals, celebrate the festivals, recite the proper formulae, and manage the property. In the texts the owner frequently specifies that he has made his tomb on a site unencumbered by earlier tombs, that he did not appropriate the tomb or building materials of another man, and that he paid his workmen in full or was granted the architectural elements of the chapel by the king. Contractual arrangements with his priests and children are also included, detailing that the endowments are to be handed over in custody from one generation to the next and not subdivided among the priests themselves, with the stipulation that a priest relinquishing his duties must also relinquish the property to another man who will carry out the duties.[15]

Although the texts occasionally include autobiographical details and even in rare instances narratives, they are usually restricted to often repeated set phrases. The chief appeal of these chapels to the present day visitor is the representation of the activities on the agricultural estate and the artistry of the draftsmen and relief sculptors who executed the reliefs. To illustrate the activities being carried out for the provisioning of the deceased owner the relief sculptor selected from a set repertory of scenes those which he or his patron preferred and which could be accommodated to his means, essentially the available wall space in the single or multiple offering chambers. Among the scenes frequently selected are those of the provision of food and drink, clothing, incense, and ointments and oils. To these are added scenes of work on the estate: the sowing, ploughing, and harvesting of barley and wheat, threshing, winnowing, and the delivery of grain, the flax harvest, the raising and care of cattle, milking, butchering, fowling and fishing, the raising of domesticated fowl, hunting in the desert and the bringing of the various desert animals to the owner (oryx, antelope, hyena, etc.). The preparation of food plays a major role: baking, brewing, cooking, and the activities of the kitchen. The workshops are shown with carpenters hewing timbers to fashion boats, beds, chairs, and a variety of furniture. Jewelers string necklaces. Leather workers prepare their hides.[16]

These scenes provide us with an insight into the details and the level of the technology of the Old Kingdom: the methods of weaving, fashioning statues, operating the furnace, growing the grape and making wine, etc. The hieroglyphic captions to the scenes provide many of the terms for the operations and introduce us to the names of the professions: the fowler, the fisherman, the butcher, the baker, the carpenter, the jeweler, the weaver, the herdsman, and many others.

There are also the officials responsible for the offering cult: the scroll bearing lector priests, the *ka*-servants, and others. In several tombs are shown the burial rites with the transportation of the deceased to the

---

[14]The history and development of the formula with its various clauses and specifications are discussed by Winfried Barta. *Aufbau und Bedeutung der altägyptischen Opferformel,* Ägyptologische Forschungen 24, J. J. Augustin, Glückstadt, 1968.

[15]Several of these texts are edited and discussed by Hans Goedicke, *Die privaten Rechtsinschriften aus dem Alten Reich,* Beihefte zur Wiener Zeitschrift für die Kunde des Morgenlandes, 5. Band, Verlag Notring, Vienna, 1970.

[16]The scenes are discussed and treated by several scholars. Of primary interest are the following: Luise Klebs, *Die Reliefs des alten Reiches (2980-2475 v. Chr.): Material zur ägyptischen Kulturgeschichte,* Abhandlungen der Heidelberger Akademie der Wissenschaften. Phil.-hist. Klasse 3, Abhandlung. Carl Winters Universitätsbuchhandlung, Heidelberg, 1915; Jacques Vandier, *Manuel d'archéologie égyptienne,* Tome II, 1: *Les grandes époques, L'architecture funéraire* (1954); Tomes IV-V, *Bas-reliefs et peintures, Scènes de la vie quotidienne* (1964, 1969), Éditions A. et J. Picard et Cie., Paris; Walter Wreszinski, *Atlas zur altägyptischen Kulturgeschichte,* Teil III: *Gräber des alten Reiches,* J. C. Hinrichs Verlag, Leipzig, 1923-1939; Rosemarie Drenkhahn, *Die Handwerker und ihre Tätigkeit im alten Ägypten,* Ägyptologische Abhandlungen 31, O. Harrassowitz, Wiesbaden, 1976.

house of embalming and thence to the tomb, the funeral procession with mourners and the text of their lamentations, and other stages involved with the burial.[17]

In many of the scenes the captions provide the conversations among the participants, the overseer giving orders, the reply of the fieldhands, an occasional jest, a warning, and the usual banter of men at work.[18]

In all these wall surfaces the owner of the tomb, the deceased, is represented on a much larger scale to emphasize his importance and almost supernatural significance. When his wife or mother is seated beside him, she shares this scale; children are usually reduced to the smaller scale. In one of the traditional scenes he is shown playing a game of draughts with his figure on the larger scale and the opponent shown on the smaller scale. In most cases he is shown passively unengaged, viewing the activities yet not participating.[19] He inspects the processions of offerings from his estates, the work in the fields and workshops, the fishermen, fowlers, butchers, and herdsmen. He carries or leans on a staff and is rarely connected to the other figures. When he is involved, it is in terms of receiving rather than participating. This passive participation is illustrated in his holding a lotus flower extended to him by his son or accepting with his hands the accounts of his produce from his steward. For this reason he is generally regarded as a deceased landlord viewing the on-going activities of the living. Rare are the scenes in which he is clearly shown during his lifetime in an actual event, such as his visit to the offering chamber in a carrying chair to inspect the work on the tomb.[20]

The essentially non-participatory figure of the owner is emphasized by the convention of his representation: the head always in profile with the eye shown full front, the torso shown full front, the hips in profile, the legs in profile with the big toe shown foremost and the toes never articulated. The right and left hands are frequently interchanged to provide a more pleasing composition.

In contrast to the representation of the passive owner, the other figures are never inactive. Each is shown actively and energetically at his assigned task: "all gestures are practical, explicative of action, not of purpose or emotion."[21] The well being of the estate is emphasized, emotion and dramatic confrontation avoided, and military activities almost never shown.

The decorative program which resulted in the completed reliefs of a mastaba offering chamber was the outcome of the plans and realization of a team of craftsmen. The selection of themes and their disposition on the walls, probably in collaboration with the client who commissioned the tomb, were the initial steps. This involved certain prescribed elements: the emplacement of the funerary formulae, the disposition of one or several "false-doors" on the west wall, the provision for the texts which contained the owner's name and the specification of his offices and ranks, and the selection of such texts as the address to the visitors, sometimes with a benediction of the visitor who recites the invocation formula and a curse upon the miscreant who damages the chapel or removes its blocks, quotations from royal letters, and legal stipulations.

---

[17]Hartwig Altenmüller, "Bestattungsritual," in *Lexikon der Ägyptologie* (ed. Wolfgang Helck and Eberhard Otto), Band I, Lieferung 5, 745-765, O. Harrassowitz, Wiesbaden 1973; John A. Wilson, "Funeral Services of the Egyptian Old Kingdom," *Journal of Near Eastern Studies* 3 (1944) 201-218; Jürgen Settgast, *Untersuchungen zu altägyptischen Bestattungsdarstellungen,* Abhandlungen des Deutschen Archäologisches Institut Abteilung Kairo 3, 1960.

[18]Adolf Erman, *Reden, Rufe, und Lieder auf Gräberbildern des alten Reiches,* Preussische Akademie der Wissenschaften. Abhandlungen, Phil.-hist. Klasse 1918, Nr. 15, Berlin, 1919; Hermann Junker, *Zu einigen Reden und Rufen auf den Grabbildern des Alten Reiches,* Sitzungsberichte der Akad. der Wiss. in Wien, 221. Band Wien-Leipzig, 1943; Pierre Montet, *Les scènes de la vie privée dans les tombeaux égyptiens de l'ancien empire.* Publications de la Faculté des Lettres de l'Université de Strasbourg, Strasbourg, 1925.

[19]H.-A. Groenewegen-Frankfort, *Arrest and Movement, An Essay on Space and Time in the representational Art of the Ancient Near East,* Faber and Faber, London, 1951, 28-36.

[20]In the tomb of Ankhmare at Giza (G 7837/7843), unpublished.

[21]H.-A. Groenewegen-Frankfort, *Arrest and Movement,* 42.

Once the selection and emplacement of these elements were settled, the outline draftsman drew the scenes and texts on the smoothed limestone surface. Following his work the relief sculptor cut back along the outlines to bring the figures and hieroglyphs into relief and carved the interior details. Finally the painter colored the reliefs with his pigments, adding details such as the beads of the necklaces, the patterning of the garments, the characteristics of materials such as the veining of stone vessels and the surface of wood, the feathering of the bird wings, and the colors of the hides of the oxen.[22]

The visitor, in ancient times as well as today, is conscious of three related matters: (1) the function of the offering chamber as the cult place of the deceased; (2) the meaning of the scenes and their identification; and (3) the relative merit of the artists who carried out the program, as compared with those of other mastaba tomb chapels. The study of the last element is still in its infancy, and further research may enable the scholar to identify several groups or schools of artisans, and to trace the originator of a scene and the stages through which the scene is altered in subsequent copies. What at first sight appears to be an original idea turns out upon investigation to be a stock element in the repertory,[23] the cow weeping at the loss of its calf, the stubble on the chin of the farmer with his pitchfork, and the man who holds the beak of a fowl so that it will not bite him.

Even within the formalized program of these representations, it seems that the artist was able to comment in his delineation of the features of the men and women as well as in the positions. The face of the tomb owner is generally treated without relevance to his age, suggesting a timeless and admittedly bland outlook. The scribe seems to show a trace of seriousness, intellect, and preoccupation (Ill. 1). The field hands have heavy features, large lips, and weak chins, and we may suspect that the artist deliberately conveyed a sense of stupidity (Ill. 2). The artist worked with stock elements for characterization: the stubble beard of the pitchfork men, the disshevelled hair of the herdsmen, the protruding stomachs of the fowlers and fishermen. Yet we can see a refinement in these characterizations in his treatment of the faces, and this line of study may also repay our efforts.

---

[22]The steps are discussed in W. Stevenson Smith, *A History of Egyptian Sculpture and Painting in the Old Kingdom,* Harvard University Press, Cambridge, 1946, 244-272; Caroline Ransom Williams, *The Decoration of the Tomb of Per-Neb: The Technique and Color Conventions,* Metropolitan Museum of Art, Department of Egyptian Art, Vol. 3, New York, 1932.

[23]Peter Seibert, *Die Charakteristik.* Teil I: *Philologische Bearbeitung der Bezeugungen,* Ägyptologische Abhandlungen 17, Otto Harrassowitz, Wiesbaden, 1967.

The Impact of the Art of Egypt
on the Art of Syria and Palestine

by

Harold A. Liebowitz
The University of Texas at Austin

The distinguished authors in this volume have naturally emphasized aspects of native Egyptian art. However, ancient Egypt's extraordinary contribution to pictorial and plastic art must also be measured by its effect on the art of the lands beyond the borders of Egypt. The art of all the lands which came into contact with the art of Egypt came under its sway and was permanently altered by it. The art of Nubia, the Levant, and to an extent, even the art of the Aegean, is imbued with the spirit and legacy of Egypt. In this paper, I would like to discuss the impact of Egyptian art on the art of the Levant.

Though I lack the space to adequately trace the course of Egyptian foreign relations with Syria-Palestine, I would like to briefly mention aspects of the history of Egyptian foreign relations with Syria-Palestine which make the aforementioned impact of Egyptian art on the art of the Levant intelligible.

There is a growing body of evidence to support the notion of Egyptian contacts with Palestine beginning in the Palestinian Chalcolithic period[1] which corresponds to the Egyptian pre-Dynastic period. These contacts continue into the Early Bronze Age[2] (c. 3200-2150 B.C.).

Yet to argue, as some have,[3] that Egyptian hegemony extended over most of Canaanite Syria-Palestine during the Old Kingdom is forcing the evidence. While military expeditions may have been sent into the Levant, they were not prompted by imperialistic aims and were of no lasting consequence.[4] Existing evidence has tempted some scholars to advocate the notion of Egyptian domination of Palestine in Middle

---

[1] Helene J. Kantor, "The Relative Chronology of Egypt and its Foreign Correlations Before the Late Bronze Age," *Chronologies in Old World Archaeology*, Robert W. Ehrich, ed., Chicago, 1965, pp. 6-7; J. B. Hennessey, *The Foreign Relations of Palestine During the Early Bronze Age*, London, 1967, pp. 26-35; see additional references cited by Ruth Amiran in "An Egyptian Jar Fragment with the Name of Narmer from Arad," *Israel Exploration Journal*, 24, 1974, p. 9, notes 25-28.

[2] R. de Vaux, "Palestine in the Early Bronze Age," *The Cambridge Ancient History*, Vol. I, Part 2: *Early History of the Middle East*, 3rd ed., Cambridge, 1971, pp. 231-233; Hennessy, *op. cit.*, 1967, pp. 49-62, 69-74. These contacts, perhaps unabated since Chalcolithic times, begin at the start of Dynasty I. Sherds with the name of King Narmer were discovered in excavations at Tell 'Erani (S. Yeivin, "Early Contacts Between Canaan and Egypt," *Israel Exploration Journal*, 10, 1960, pp. 193-203) and more recently at Tell Arad (Amiran, *op. cit.*, 1974, pp. 4-12).

[3] W. F. Albright, "The Role of the Canannites in the History of Civilization," *Studies in the History of Culture: The Discipline of the Humanities*, Percy W. Long, ed., Menasha, Wisconsin, 1942, p. 16; cf. Ram Gophna, "Excavations at 'En Besor," *Aitiqot* 11 (1976), pp. 1-9.

[4] John A. Wilson, *The Culture of Ancient Egypt*, 9th ed., Chicago, 1963, p. 82.

Kingdom times.[5] Egypt, however, does not appear to have had a strong economic or political influence, or exercised political control over Palestine even at this time. Indeed Egyptian contacts with Palestine were expanded at the end of the Middle Bronze IIA period, but that expansion comes precisely at the eve of the Egyptian collapse at the beginning of the Hyksos period.[6] On the other hand, the Egyptian domination of Syria-Palestine in New Kingdom times is well documented. With the victory of Tuthmosis III at Megiddo, Syria-Palestine was brought under Egyptian hegemony.[7] Though Egyptian control of Palestine and Syria was lessened during the Amarna Age, the region, particularly Palestine, remained under the control of Egypt throughout the fourteenth century.[8] Egypt's control of Palestine waned through the course of the Ramesside Age. While Rameses III managed to retain his holding in Western Asia, there is no clear evidence that Egypt retained her dependencies in Palestine and Syria after his death.[9] Egyptian relations with Palestine were resumed during the reign of Solomon as evidenced by the biblical evidence of Solomon's marriage to the daughter of pharaoh[10] and the commercial relations of both states.[11] Egypt assumed an aggressive military policy towards Palestine following the death of Solomon in 931/930. In 925 Shishak I, the founder of Dynasty XXII, swept through Judah and Israel destroying numerous cities and marching off with the wealth of both kingdoms.[12] Though the victory may have established Shishak as the overlord of Palestine, we were told neither of further Egyptian incursions into Palestine nor of any interference in the affairs of either Judah or Israel.

As a result of these contacts through the ages, Palestinian craftsmen had ample opportunity to familiarize themselves with Egyptian art. While some Levantine craftsmen may have visited Egypt, it is more likely that they familiarized themselves with the art of Egypt through the presence of examples of Egyptian minor arts in Syria-Palestine, which were found in increasing numbers from the Chalcolithic period to the new Kingdom.

I would like to proceed with a presentation of a sampling of the evidence which illustrates the enormity of the impact of the art of Egypt on the art of Palestine and Syria.[13] The earliest examples of genres of locally made Palestinian and Syrian art objects with obvious Egyptian affinities date to the Middle Bronze Age (c. 2150-1550).

---

[5]W. F. Albright, *The Archaeology of Palestine,* 6th ed., Baltimore, 1961, p. 74; Wolfgang Helck, *Die Beziehungen Ägyptens zu Vorderasien um 3. und 2. Jahrtausend v. Chr.* (Ägyptologische Abhandlungen, Bd. 5), Weisbaden, 1962, p. 69; B. Mazar, "The Middle Bronze Age in Palestine," *Israel Exploration Journal* 18, 1968, pp. 71-75.

[6]For a recent, full discussion of the question, see: James M. Weinstein, "Egyptian Relations with Palestine in the Middle Kingdom," *Bulletin of the American Schools of Oriental Research,* 217, 1975, pp. 1-4. Cf. William C. Hayes, "The Middle Kingdom in Egypt," *The Cambridge Ancient History,* Vol. I, Part 2: *Early History of the Middle East,* 3rd ed., Cambridge, 1971, pp. 500, 501, 508.

[7]Wilson, *op. cit.,* 1963, pp. 167-86; George Steindorff and Keith C. Seele, *When Egypt Ruled the East,* 2nd ed., 4th impression, Chicago, 1965, pp. 53-66; Margaret S. Drower, "Syria c. 1550-1400 B.C.," *The Cambridge Ancient History:* Vol. II, Part 1: *The Middle East and the Aegean Region,* 3rd ed., Cambridge, 1973, pp. 444-62.

[8]Cyril Aldred, "Egypt: The Amarna Period and the End of the Eighteenth Dynasty," *The Cambridge Ancient History:* Vol. II, Part 2, *The Middle East and the Aegean Region,* 3rd ed., Cambridge, 1975, pp. 81-86. Cf. William C. Hayes, *The Scepter of Egypt,* II: *The Hyksos Period and the New Kingdom* (1675-1080), Cambridge, 1959, pp. 280, 281, 295; Wilson, *op. cit.,* 1963, pp. 230-31; Steindorff and Seele, *op. cit.,* 1965, pp. 80-81.

[9]J. Černy, "Egypt: From the Death of Ramesses III to the End of the Twenty-first Dynasty," *The Cambridge Ancient History,* Vol. II, Part 2: *The Middle East and the Aegean Region,* 3rd ed., Cambridge, 1975, pp. 614-15.

[10]I Kings 3:1.

[11]I Kings 10:28.

[12]I Kings 14:25, 26; see also K. A. Kitchen, *The Third Intermediate Period in Egypt* (1100-650), Warminster, England, 1973, pp. 294-96. The dates follow Kitchen's chronology.

[13]A headless, female ivory figurine discovered in the Chalcolithic level of Bir Safadi, near Beer-sheba (Jean Perrot, "La 'Venus' de Beerheva," *Eretz-Israel,* 9, 1969, pp. 100-01, pl. XIII) closely parallels a female ivory figurine discovered in

Let us first examine several stelae from the Syrian coastal site of Ras Shamra, ancient Ugarit. The stelae from Ugarit are carved on one face, and feature a single standing deity which fills practically the entire vertical space of the stelae. The basic stance of the Resheph figure, which dominates the stelae commonly called the Baal au Foudre[14] (Ill. 1) from Niveau II, and dated by Schaeffer to 1900-1750 B.C., harks back to the classic stance of the pharaoh smiting his enemies. This motif is found on the Narmer Palette[15] and continues in the Egyptian repertoire into the Middle Kingdom, where it is found on a pectoral of Amenemhet III (1842-1797)[16] and on royal reliefs of the New Kingdom.

However, the Syrian figure differs from the Egyptian prototype in the choice of attributes. The spiked and horned helmet and the curled locks of the Syrian figure[17] are absent on the Egyptian prototypes. The figure also differs stylistically from the Egyptian prototypes in the way in which the back of the legs arch out, a feature characteristic of Hittite sculpture.[18] The proportions of the body also lack the balance achieved in Egyptian statuary and relief.[19] Furthermore, in contrast with Egyptian relief, which has modeled surfaces, the relief on the Ugarit stelae is flat and lacking in detail.

The subsidiary motif on the Ugarit stelae, a figure standing on a pedestal, with its right arm bent at the elbow and raised in front of the face, while the left arm and hand are lowered and covered by the cloak, is Egyptian in character. But, the treatment of the motif finds its closest comparison in an LB I bronze plaque from Hazor.[20]

---

a grave of the Badarian period in Egypt (G. Brunton, G. Caton-Thompson, *The Badarian Civilization*, London, 1928, pl. XXIV.2). The figurines are similar in the daring treatment of the arms, which are separated from the torso, in the stylized placement of the hands on the waist, in the separation of the legs, in the bend of the knees and the stylization of the feet, and in the treatment and placement of the breasts and the emphasis on the pubic triangle. The ivories differ in that only the Palestinian figure is featured as pregnant. Moreover, while the head of the Palestinian example is missing, on the basis of similar Palestinian ivories of the same period, it may be safely assumed that whereas the eyes of the Egyptian example are incised, the eyes of the Palestinian example were inlaid. Nevertheless, the parallel is significant. While the Palestinian example is typical of a number of other Chalcolithic Palestinian ivories (cf. Perrot, "Statuettes en ivoire et autres objects en ivoire et en os provenant des gisements prehistoriques de la region de Beersheva," *Syria*, 36, 1959, pp. 8-9, pls. II, III), the Egyptian example is not typical of other known Badarian figurines. I am therefore inclined to consider the possibility that the Egyptian example is an import from Palestine. Therefore, I do not cite this parallel as evidence in support of Palestinian dependency on Egyptian art.

[14]C. F. A. Schaeffer, *Ugaritica II*, Paris, 1939, pp. 121-30, pls. XXIII, XXIV. Schaeffer identifies the figure as Baal on the basis of literary analogies, but is puzzled by the absence of the bull, the animal attribute of Baal (*Ugaritica* II, p. 127). It is more likely that the figure can be identified with Resheph. See, Sarah B. Jones, *Resheph Statuettes from Syria and Palestine*, unpublished M.A. thesis, New York University, 1966, p. 42.

[15]Schaeffer, *op. cit.*, 1939-, p. 123

[16]Cyril Aldred, *Middle Kingdom Art in Egypt*, pl. 73. Here, however, the pose is slightly different, since the pharaoh bends forward somewhat. But the motif is basically the same. See also the Dynasty XI wall painting depicting a figure grasping the tail of a bull with his left hand, while he holds a branch in his raised right hand, about to strike the animal (W. Stevenson Smith, *The Art and Architecture of Ancient Egypt*, Baltimore, 1965, pl. 58-B).

[17]These attributes are paralleled on a cylinder seal attributed by Porada to her second Syrian Group (Edith Porada, ed., *Corpus of Ancient Near Eastern Seals in North American Collections*, New York, 1948, pl. CXLVI. 964) and by a cylinder seal from Tell el-Ajjul (Flinders Petrie, *Ancient Gaza*, IV, London, 1931-1952, pl. XII.2) of uncertain date, but which probably dates to the Late Bronze Age.

[18]Henri Frankfort, *The Art and Architecture of the Ancient Orient*, Baltimore, 1963, pls. 127, 129-A.

[19]The left leg is more substantial than the right leg, the head is too large for the body, the chest is exceptionally small, and the right arm is awkwardly joined to the shoulder.

[20]Yigael Yadin, *et. al.*, Hazor I, Jerusalem, 1958, pl. CCXXXIX.1,2; See also Briggs, Buchanan, *Catalogue of Ancient Near Eastern Cylinder Seals in the Ashmolean Museum of Ancient Near Eastern Cylinder Seals*, Vol. I, Oxford, 1966. The seal is included in his section on seals of his Old Syrian Style. He notes that seals of this type have been called Hyksos (*Ibid.* p. 177).

The pose of the goddess with the feathered robe[21] and the god with the stylized tree projecting from his head[22] on two additional stelae from Niveau II is common on Egyptian statuary and relief. Egyptian figures, with the right arm at the side and the left arm bent at the elbow and slightly extended, usually hold a staff in the extended and raised hand. The pose is perhaps the most popular in the Egyptian repertoire.[23] But, once again note the differences in the choice of attributes. The gods on the Ugarit stelae carry lances in place of the more usual staff of the Egyptian prototypes.

A comparison of the treatment of the legs of the male figure with the legs of the female figure on the two latter stelae provides additional evidence for coastal Syrian dependency on Egyptian prototypes. As in Egyptian prototypes,[24] the stride of the male figure is obviously longer than that of the female.

There are also iconographic points of comparison between these Ugarit stelae and Egyptian art. The god holds the crook of Osiris in his right hand, and the diagonal projection ending in a coil emerging from his forehead recalls an element of the crown of Lower Egypt.[25] However, the other attributes of the gods, such as the lances, the scabbard attached to the god's belt, the stylized tree coiffure, the torque and the short kilt on the god, and the sandals on both the god and goddess on the stelae from Ugarit succeed in recasting the figure into a native coastal Syrian iconographic representation.

In the Middle Bronze Age, numerous examples of human figurines in metal were found in coastal Syria at Ugarit, Tell Sukas, Tell Simiryan and Byblos; relatively few examples were found further inland at Alalakh and at Hama; and a fair number were found in Northern Palestine at Nahariyah, Megiddo and Beth Shan.

Elsewhere, I have divided the Palestinian and Syrian Middle Bronze Age bronzes into fifteen distinct types.[26] With the exception of a stone mold for figurines found at Tell Sukas, Type I to VIII are found exclusively at Byblos.[27] The motifs of these Byblos figurines are for the most part inspired by Egyptian prototypes with varying degrees of modification in the stylistic treatment. The figurines conforming most closely to the Egyptian prototypes in stance, wig type, facial treatment, and style are represented by those of Type IB.[28]

---

[21] Schaeffer, *op. cit.,* 1939, pl. XXII.1. and pp. 89,90.

[22] *Ibid.,* pl. XXII.2. and pp. 90-93.

[23] Examples are numerous. A few characteristic examples from the Old Kingdom, the First Intermediate Period, and the Middle Kingdom will suffice. An example in relief is found in the Dynasty IV offering niche of Iynefer (Smith, *op. cit.,* 1965, pl. 28-A); an example in wood sculpture is found in the fifth dynasty statue of the Province Administration Mitry (William C. Hayes, *The Scepter of Egypt,* Vol. I, New York, 1953, Fig. 64). An example in relief from the First Intermediate Period is found on a painted limestone stela in Philadelphia (Smith, *op. cit.,* 1965, pl. 28-A); an example in wood sculpture from the same period occurs on a statue from Assiut (*Ibid.,* pl. 56-B). There are two wooden Dynasty XII statues of Senusret I (*Ibid.,* pl. 65-B). A painted limestone relief of courtiers bringing offerings to Senusret I depicts a variation on the motif where in place of the staff in the extended left hand, the hand is used to balance a basket on the courtier's left shoulder (Hayes, *op. cit.,* 1953, fig. 114).

[24] Compare the two male courtiers in the mortuary temple of Senusret I at Lisht (Hayes, *op. cit.,* 1953, fig. 114, p. 186) with the daughters of Thuthotpe on a painted relief fragment from Bersheh (Smith, *op. cit.,* 1965, pl. 74-A).

[25] Cyril Aldred, *Middle Kingdom Art in Ancient Egypt,* London, 1956, pl. 16.

[26] Harold A. Liebowitz, *Regionalism in the Art of Syria and Palestine in the Middle Bronze Age,* Ann Arbor, 1972, pp. 136, 148 (University Microfilms, Ph.D. Dissertation).

[27] *Ibid.,* p. 149.

[28] There are very few copper and bronze statuettes from Middle Kingdom Egypt. Several purchased examples dated stylistically to the Middle Kingdom were published by Hall. See the copper figurine in the Fitzwilliam Museum at Cambridge dated by Hall to Dynasty XI-XII (H. R. Hall, "Some Early Copper and Bronze Egyptian Figurines," *Liverpool Annals of Archaeology and Anthropology,* 16, 1929, pl. XII-A-C, and p. 16). Note also the Dynasty VI statue of Pepy I (Kazimierz Michalowski, *Art of Ancient Egypt,* trans. and adapted from the Polish and the French by Norbert Guterman, New York, 1968, fig. 232, p. 366) and the Dynasty VI copper statuette of Merenre (Smith, *op. cit.,*

The figurines of Type IA also accord well in stance and in spirit with Egyptian prototypes,[29] although the essential flatness of the torso and the treatment of the facial features are un-Egyptian. Perhaps the finest statuette from Byblos,[30] from Deposit (14433-14500), belonging to Type IA, represents the most fully developed example of the type. However, even this example, in spite of its fine modeling, is relatively flat, elongated, and lacks the mass and volume associated with Egyptian statuary.[31]

Silhouette figurines cut from sheet bronze, gold or silver comprise my Type VIII.[32] The poses struck by these figurines are often borrowed from the Egyptian repertoire. Figurines of this type, from the Obelisk temple at Byblos, recall one of the typical Egyptian figure stances, though the genre of the flat, metal silhouettes is atypical of Egypt. However, recent excavations of the structure formerly called the Pyramid of Mentuhotep II yielded figures crudely cut from sheet bronze similar in style to some of the Type VIII figurines.[33] In spite of the fact that the Egyptian examples stand on pliths, the association is significant and permits a dating of some of the undated Byblos figures of Type VIII to the reign of Mentuhotep II (2060-2010 B.C.).

The Middle Bronze II strata in Palestine, and to a lesser extent in coastal Syria, are characterized by the presence of decorated bone strips and silhouettes applied to wooden boxes. The bone strips are primarily decorated with geometric motifs and the silhouettes primarily include birds rendered with interior incised details. While, as I have argued elsewhere, the genre is indigenous to Palestine[34] and the decorated bone strips and silhouettes from Sedment in Egypt are probably imports, several bone strips and silhouettes are decorated with Egyptianizing elements.

A remarkable group of silhouettes, apparently correctly identified by their excavator as ivory,[35] was found in a Middle Bronze II tomb near el-Jisr in Palestine.[36] These silhouettes differ considerably from the bone silhouettes discussed above in the expanded repertoire of motifs, such as human figures and lions; in the more naturalistic style; and in the Egyptianizing tendencies, seen most emphatically in the dress, positioning of the limbs, and style of the male and female figure (Ill. 2), and in aspects of the manner of treatment of the animals.

The greater interest in naturalism is reflected in the more life-like contours and in the more true-to-life treatment of details. The eyes, for example, are not rendered as dotted circles, but rather as naturalistic organs seen frontally as in Egyptian, Mesopotamian, and Aegean art. The naturalistic tendencies of the

---

1965, pl. 53-B), the Dynasty VI wooden statue of Methethy (Aldred, *op. cit.*, 1956, pl. 59) and the painted and inscribed early Middle Kingdom statuettes of the Scribe of the Divine Offerings, Merer (Hayes, *op. cit.*, 1953, fig. 129, p. 212).

[29] Cf. the wooden Dynasty VI statue of the Overseer of the Granary, Kaemsenwy (Hayes, *op. cit.*, 1953, fig. 66, p. 113) and the twin painted wooden statues of Senusret I (Aldred, *op. cit.*, 1956, pl. 20).

[30] Maurice Dunand, *Byblos*, II, Paris, 1954, pl. CXV.144467.

[31] Cf. Donald P. Hansen, "Some Remarks on the Chronology and Style of Objects from Byblos," *AJA*, 73, 1969, p. 284.

[32] Dunand, *op. cit.*, 1954, pl. CXXVII.15023.

[33] Dieter Arnold, "Sechster Vorbericht über die vom Deutschen Archaologischen Institut Kairo in Qurna unternommenen Arbeiten (8. Kampagne)," *MDAIK*, 27, 1971, pp. 125-30, pl. XXII, 11, 12, 14.

[34] See abstract of paper delivered at the General Meeting of the Archaeological Institute of America, 15 December, 1971, *AJA*, 76, 1972, p. 214; cf. Liebowitz, *op. cit.*, 1972, pp. 329-33.

[35] Since with this possible single exception there is not attestation of the use of ivory by Palestinian craftsmen in the Middle Bronze Age I considered these silhouettes bone. Cf. Helene Kantor, *JNES*, 15, 1956, p. 158. However, for a recent opinion that they are ivory, see Ruth Amiran, *Israel Museum News* 12 (1977), pp. 65-69.

[36] J. Ory, "A Middle Bronze Age Tomb at el-Jisr," *Quarterly of the Department of Antiquities of Palestine*, 12, 1945, 6, pp. 31-42.

el-Jisr examples are also seen by comparing the bone silhouettes of quadrupeds from Megiddo[37] with the ivory silhouettes of cows from el-Jisr.[38]   In addition to the more naturalistic treatment of the contour and the eyes of the bulls, note the detailed rendering of the tail and its attachment to the hind-quarters.   On the other hand, a stylized treatment of natural features is represented by the curved incised line extending from the upper edge of the forward line of the right foreleg to the upper edge of the forequarters.   This feature occurs on animals in the Egyptian Twelfth Dynasty tomb of Senbi, son of Ukhotpe at Meir.[39] The frontal rendering of the horns also accords with Egyptian style.

The standing male human figures are rendered in the Egyptian tradition with the head and legs in profile and the eyes and shoulders frontal.   The contours of the slim male figures are carefully cut and attention is given to inner detail.

The female figure[40] stands with her right arm at her side and her left arm bent at the elbow with her left forearm and hand placed diagonally across her chest in a traditional Egyptian pose.[41]   The long garment worn by the figure is also characteristic of Egyptian female apparel, except that the manner in which the garment billows out in front of her is notably un-Egyptian.

Two bone strips from Tell Beit Mirsim D, MB IIC (ca. 1600-1550)[42] are decorated not with the usual geometric motifs, but with a running fawn incised on each strip.   The fawn on the larger strip faces left towards an obliquely placed stylized bush (Ill. 3).   The fawn on the smaller strip faces right, towards the left side of a vertically placed stylized bush at the right edge of the strip.   The legs of the fawns are stretched out in front and back and are firmly placed on the ground in a conventional Egyptian running attitude.   The outlines of the fawn are angular, but relatively naturalistic, as opposed to the stylization of the bone bird silhouettes.   The pose, with the hindlegs and the forelegs stretched out, is seen on a dog and on long-horned antelopes on the east wall of the slightly earlier Twelfth Dynasty tomb chapel of Senbi's son Ukhotpe at Meir.[43]   The legs of the two long-horned animals on the Meir relief[44] are bent as are the legs of the fawns on the Tell Beit Mirsim inlay.   However, the bend in the legs on the Palestinian example is far more extreme.

A second example of this genre manifesting Egyptian influence is represented by a bone strip depicting a male prisoner in a long robe.[45]   This strip, found in the First Palace at Tell el-Ajjul, probably dates to late MB IIB or MB IIC[46] and is, therefore, essentially contemporary with the examples from Tell Beit Mrisim.   The standing male prisoner dressed in a long robe fills the entire vertical space, as do the fawns on the Tell Beit Mirsim examples.   The long robe on the figure is characteristic of Asiatic dress at the beginning of the second

---

[37]*Megiddo,* II, pl. 193:4; 194:12.

[38]Ory, *op. cit.,* 1945, pl. XIV, 83, 84, 86.

[39]Aylward Blackman, *The Rock Tombs of Meir,* I: *The Tomb Chapel of Ukh-Hotp's Son Senbi,* London, 1914, pl. VI.

[40]Ory, *op, cit.,* 1945, pl. XIV, 71.

[41]This pose is found already in the Dynasty III statue of Sepa (Smith, *op. cit.,* 1965, pl. 23).

[42]W. F. Albright, *The Excavations of Tell Beit Mirsim,* Vol. II: *The Bronze Age,* AASOR, Vol. XVII, New Haven, 1938, pl. 34.

[43]Blackman, *op. cit.,* 1914, pl. VI.

[44]*Idem.* One long-horned animal is facing right with a spear through its foreparts, and another, to its left, is being attacked by a dog.

[45]Petrie, *op. cit.,* 1931-1952, pl. XXIV.

[46]A date of late seventeenth-early sixteenth century B.C. was proposed for Palace I both by Albright (*AJSL,* 55, 1938, pp. 348-50, chart p. 359) and Kathleen Kenyon ("Palestine in the Middle Bronze Age," p. 28).

millennium, as indicated by the Twelfth Dynasty painting in the tomb of Khnumhotpe at Beni Hasan depicting a group of Semites on their way to Egypt.[47]

The garment is filled with short vertical incisions similar to the filling motif on the bodies of the dogs, the lion, and the antelopes on the underside of a game box from a Theban Seventeenth Dynasty burial.[48] The late Second Intermediate period date of the Theban example accords with the late MBII date suggested for the Tell el-Ajjul incised strip.

The cylinder seals represent yet another area in which Egyptian artistic influence is manifested, albeit limited. Confronting male figures striking Egyptian stances, and with *ankh* signs serving as filling motifs, are found in Palestine and Syria, for example, on a cylinder from Tell Beit Mirsim[49] and on a seal from Ras Shamra (Ill. 4).[50] A seal impression from Alalakh features, in addition to the *ankh* sign to the left of the central figures, an Egyptian sun disc to the right of the central figures above four smaller figures with identical poses.[51] A fragmentary sealing from Tell Mardikh in inland Syria which may possibly have featured a similar composition to the Alalakh seal, also has an *ankh* sign and a winged sun disc.[52]

The Late Bronze Age ushers us into the period which may be called the High Renaissance of Palestinian art. Late Bronze Age strata yield examples of orthostats, stone sculpture in the round, bronze figurines, and elaborate cylinder seals. However, the artistic spirit of the age is perhaps best represented by the ivories, which represent, in my opinion, the major achievement of Palestinian and Syrian art.

In the realm of bone and ivory work, three major changes occurred in the Late Bronze Age. Ivory replaced bone, relief carving largely replaced incised drawing, and complex compositions replaced the individual motifs characteristic of the Middle Bronze Age. In addition to these internal developments in the art of the period, the art of the Levant in the Late Bronze Age is characterized by a spirit of internationalism. The foreign influences on the art of Syria and Palestine range from Egypt to the Aegean and Anatolia. Nevertheless, the strongest influence is exerted by the art of Egypt. Its impact is felt both in motif and style.

The borrowed motifs include, among others, a recumbent winged sphinx, such as the one seen on an ivory openwork plaque from Megiddo VIIA,[53] which is paralleled by a recumbent winged sphinx on a bracelet of Queen Tiy the wife of Amenhotep III.[54] While the similarity between the winged sphinx on the Megiddo ivory and the winged sphinx on the bracelet is evident, the uniqueness of the Canaanite style is apparent in the fanciful headdress on the Palestinian example and in the substitution of a meaningless cup for the cartouche in the Egyptian example.

---

[47]Percy E. Newberry, *Beni Hasan I,* "Archaeological Survey of Egypt," F. L. Griffith, ed., London, 1893, pl. XXX.

[48]Hayes, *op.cit.,* 1959, fig. 10, p. 25. The lower edge of the garment, which is formed by two tangent arcs, is thoroughly un-Egyptian. This treatment of the lower edge of the garment is found in the Aegean in the Late Bronze Age. Examples of the type are found on the mainland in the Mycenean period on a Procession Frescoe in the House of Kadmos in Thebes (Emily Vermeule, *Greece in the Bronze Age,* Chicago, 1965, pl. XXVII), and in the Late Minoan Palace III Period; however, this treatment of the garment does not occur in the Aegean in the Middle Bronze Age.

[49]Albright, *op. cit.,* 1938, pl. 30.1, 3.

[50]Claude Schaeffer, *Stratigraphie comparée et chronologie de l'Asie occidentale* (III et II² millenaires). *Syrie, Palestine, Asie Mineure, Chypre, Perse et Caucase,* Oxford, 1948, fig. 5, pl. 31.

[51]Leonard Woolley, *Alalakh: An Account of the Excavations at Tell Atchana in the Hatay,* 1937-1949, Oxford, 1955, pl. LX.9.

[52]Giorgio Castellino, *et. al., Missione Archeologica Italiana in Siria: Rapporto Preliminare Della Campagna,* 1965 (Tell Mardikh) Rome, 1966, pl. LXXIX 3,4.

[53]Gordon Loud, *The Megiddo Ivories,* Chicago, 1939, pl. 7, 22.

[54]Hayes, *op. cit.,* 1959, fig. 147, p. 243.

Egyptian elements are also evident in the ivories with complex compositions. The Egyptian elements in these hybridized ivories provide opportunities for dating that have not been fully utilized. For example, three ivory objects in various states of preservation, which feature aspects of military and feast scenes, can be securely dated on the basis of comparisons with dated Egyptian objects.

Among the ivories found in the Megiddo VIIA treasury room is an ivory plaque featuring a military and feast scene (Ill. 5).[55] While the archaeological data has been utilized to establish the terminal date for stratum VIIA at around 1150 B.C., some of the ivories could have been made earlier.

Both Henri Frankfort and William F. Albright cited the plaque as a reflection of the impact of Egyptian art on the art of the Levant. Yet each suggested a different date for the production of the ivory. Albright stated that this particular ivory was representative of ivories made during the first half of the 12th century and dated it to around 1150 B.C. or possibly earlier. Frankfort on the other hand suggested "a fourteenth century date, for in the Ramesside times Egyptian motifs seem to have been more slavishly imitated." In view of the controversy it appeared that a detailed stylistic analysis was required to establish a more accurate date.

The plaque shares various iconographic and stylistic features with Egyptian representations. The most salient iconographic parallel is with the depictions of horses hitched to chariots. In a study of nonrearing horses hitched to wheeled vehicles in Egyptian art, I noticed that three distinct phases in the treatment of horses' legs can be distinguished in New Kingdom art:

> (1) The pre-Amarna Phase in which the horses are depicted with all four legs on the ground. The forelegs are spread apart forming a narrow-based isosceles triangle, and the hindlegs are similarly treated.

> (2) The Amarna Phase, during which time the forelegs are placed together and thrust slightly forward, and the hindlegs are in a similar position.

> (3) And the Ramesside Phase, which is characterized by two outstanding features. First, the treatment of the hind legs is similar to that in the pre-Amarna phase, but the treatment of the forelegs is entirely new. One foreleg is straight and touches the ground, practically perpendicular to it, and the other is brought forward and lifted in a ceremonial-like stance. The second feature is the position of the near leg; it, rather than the far leg, is brought forward in the majority of instances.

The Megiddo plaque can be dated with certainty to the Ramesside period on the basis of the similarity between the treatment of the legs of the horses on the Megiddo ivory and the treatment of horses' legs portrayed in Ramesside times in Egypt. Not only is one leg almost perpendicular to the ground and the other brought forward and lifted, but the leg brought forward is the near leg, a stylistic detail which first occurs with regularity during the Ramesside period. The horses on the Megiddo plaque correspond most closely with the horses on a relief on a wall of the Temple of Ramesses II at Abydos, dated to the fifth year of his reign.

Trotting horses also appear in two additional ivories form the Megiddo hoard; one depicting the heat of battle and the other depicting the victorious march home. I initially dated these bars also to the Ramesside

---

[55]For a full discussion of this ivory and for the evidence upon which the stylistic conclusions are based see Harold
   A. Liebowitz, "Horses in New Kingdom Art and the Date of an Ivory from Megiddo," *Journal of the American Research Center in Egypt*, VI, 1967, pp. 129-34.

period on the basis of the treatment of the horses' legs, yet I noted the existence of somewhat troublesome parallels to Amarna art: the treatment of the fallen warriors on one of the ivory bars recalls the treatment of fallen warriors on Tutankhamun's painted box, and the posture of the attendants on the feast scene on another of the ivory bars recalls the posture of attendants in Amarna wall decoration.[56] I therefore suggested that these ivory bars dated to a very early phase of the Ramesside period. In retrospect, I am more inclined to date these bars to a late phase of the Amarna period or the Post Amarna period (Late Dynasty XVIII) because of the aforementioned parallels to the art of the Amarna period and since the treatment of the horses' legs still retain qualities more in keeping with the art of the Amarna period.[57]

The motif of the feast scene is also featured on ivory fragments from Tell el-Fara (South). One fragment depicts the hunting of provisions for the feast (Ill. 6), and the other depicts the seated prince at his victory celebration (Ill. 7). The scene with the gathering of provisions on the ivory is paralleled by a similar scene on a late Nineteenth Dynasty silver bowl[58] found near the temple of the goddess Bubastis in the eastern Delta. These ivory fragments from Tell el-Fara are generally considered undatable with any precision. However, one additional Egyptian feature permits the establishment of a date for the production of the ivory. Note the garments worn by the seated prince and his attendants. They wear ankle-length and elbow-length pleated garments and are bedecked with bread-collar necklaces. While the general style of the garment is Syro-Palestinian, the elbow-length pleated sleeves recalls the somewhat shorter version of the fashion, current in Egypt during the reign of Horemheb, as can be seen on the statue of Horemheb seated as a scribe.[59] Thus, the earliest conceivable date for this ivory is the reign of Horemheb, the first king of the Nineteenth Dynasty, who reigned in the second half of the 14th century.[59a]

The first few centuries of the Iron Age represent a dark age for Palestine and coastal Syria from the perspective of the art historian. First, beginning with the ivories of the 9th and 8th centuries B.C. from Samaria in northern Israel, and Arslan Tash in Syria, we witness the revival of Palestinian and coastal Syrian art. When the new age dawns, Egypt once again serves as the dominant influence. The Egyptianizing ivories from Syria-Palestine fall into two categories: openwork plaques decorated with figures in relief, and reliefs on solid plaques. Objects of the latter category are often decorated with inlay of insets placed in deeply grooved settings. The openwork plaques are decorated with hybrid Egyptian and Syro-Palestinian elements: as for example, the Levantine cherub, who in the Iron Age wears the Egyptian double crown and is set in a Nilotic environment (Ill. 8). The reliefs on solid plaques are very close in style to the Egyptian originals from which they were borrowed, and are sometimes difficult to distinguish from true Egyptian works of art. Indeed, the slavish imitation of Egyptian prototypes is one characteristic of the ivory carving of the Iron Age.

A second Iron Age art form which is strongly influenced by the art of Egypt is represented by the numerous scarabs and scaraboids which begin to make their appearance in the 8th century.[60] The Egyptian influence is apparent not only in the beatle shape of the scarab back, but also in the Egyptian motifs and figure style with which the intaglio bases are decorated. One example of a scarab with Egyptianizing motifs on the base may suffice to demonstrate the impact of the Egyptian art on the genre. While the lower half of one of the seals bears the inscription "Belonging to Eshna the Servant of Ahaz," in Paleo-Hebrew, the upper half is decorated with Egyptian symbols.

---

[56]*Ibid.*, p. 134, n. 50.

[57]The warlike atmosphere in Palestine during the Amarna age is likely to have encouraged the revival of the combined motifs of military and feasts scenes, already known from Mesopotamian Early Dynastic times (cf. Frankfort, *op. cit.*, 1963, pls. 36, 37).

[58]Hayes, *op. cit.*, 1959, fig. 226, p. 359.

[59]*Ibid.*, fig. 190, p. 305.

[59a]In a recently completed manuscript I adduce evidence to support a mid-14th century date for the ivory, around the reign of King Ay.

[60]A. Reifenberg, *Ancient Hebrew Seals*, London, 1950.

The Palestinian and Phoenician seals differ significantly from their Egyptian prototypes since they characteristically provide the name of the owner of the seal. Nevertheless, the Egyptian influence is evident.

The foregoing evidence supports the conclusion that the impact of Egyptian art on the art of Palestine and coastal Syria was considerable. Given the historical situation which existed in the region, the result is not surprising. However, this student of the area is surprised by the virtual restriction of the impact of Egypt on the Levant to the realm of art. The poetic imagery of Ugaritic and Biblical texts, Canaanite and Israelite attitudes towards government, Levantine cultic ritual, and the Israelite legal traditions do not reflect a commensurate Egyptian influence. I am not certain that I can fully account for this phenomenon. But I think that two related factors are relevant to the question. One is that, for reasons which I cannot go into in this paper, Palestine and Syria never created an independent iconography, and were, therefore, prepared to adopt a ready-made artistic language, much in the same way as the Akkadians adopted the written script of the Sumerians. Secondly, I believe that the Syro-Palestinians did not necessarily adopt the mythological associations along with the imagery. The Syro-Palestinian craftsmen may very well have borrowed the ready made Egyptian imagery and put it in the service of indigenous western asiatic religious conceptions, for whether the Samaria ivories were carved by Israelite craftsmen, as they very well may have been, or whether they represent Phoenician imports, it is noteworthy that the Biblical authors, while noting the opulence of the "ivory house" of Omri, did not take exception to the flagrant paganism of the symbolism. Be that as it may, the debt of Palestinian and Syrian art is immeasurable.

Tin and the Egyptian Bronze Age

by

Theodore A. Wertime
Smithsonian Institution

The picture of ancient tin everywhere has been changed in one fell swoop by a reconnaissance in the Eastern desert of Egypt in December, 1976. There a team inspected three mines of cassiterite.[1] All three of these offered placer cassiterite in a form immediately evident to the prospector. At the third, Gebel Mueilha, M. F. El-Ramly of the Egyptian Geological Survey has found eight inscriptions dating to Pepi II of the 22nd century B.C. suggesting a deliberate working of this area for tin ores.

In addition, in 1976 there were two separate finds of tin ingots, one of two Cypro-Minoan ingots off the coast of Israel, the other of a single, probably not ancient, ingot off the coast of Saudi Arabia.

I might add that there was at least one Nubian source of cassiterite lying on the sixth cataract of the Nile, in Sudan, similar to those in the granites of Egypt. I came across this on my January 1977 visit with members of the Geological Survey of the Sudan and the staff in geology at Khartoum University.[2] This adds to the suggestion that gold-bearing quartzes along the Red Sea introduced the ancient Egyptians to placer cassiterite.

Let us take a brief look at this substance tin, both as a metal and as an ore.[3] Heavy and bright, easily melted but not easily reduced from the ore, its atomic number is 50 and its atomic weight 118.69. With 10 isotopes, it has the largest number of any element, posing problems for isotopic finger-printing. It is rarer than the element hafnium in the earth's crust, appearing as the final phase of precipitation in certain granites.

Tin lies in the belt of granites running from Yunnan province in China down the Malaysian peninsula to Tasmania; in Europe in England, France, Spain, Saxony, Czechoslovakia, and Italy; in South America in Bolivia; and in Africa in Egypt, the Sudan, Nigeria, and the Congo. It does *not* appear in the granites of western North America, the Canadian Shield, Brazil, South Africa, West Australia, the Urals, and Siberia. In the ancient Middle East then, tin for the most part was not a mainstream geological phenomenon.

Egypt, as noted by Alfred Lucas, is the home of perhaps the most consistent archeological application of the metal from the Eighteenth Dynasty or Late Bronze Age onward.[4] There were such items as a ring and

---

[1] W. F. Hume. 1937. *Geology of Egypt.* Vol. II, Part III. *The Minerals of Economic Value.* (Cairo: Government Press), p. 856. Participants in the inspection team were James D. Muhly, George Rapp, and Theodore A. Wertime.

[2] A. J. Whiteman. 1971. *The Geology of the Sudan Republic.* (Oxford: Clarendon Press), pp. 246-47.

[3] Rhodes W. Fairbridge. 1972. *The Encyclopedia of Geochemistry and Environmental Sciences.* (New York: Van Nostrand), pp. 1191-92.

[4] Alfred Lucas. 1934. *Ancient Egyptian Materials and Industries.* (London: Arnold), p. 209ff.. Lucas lists a ring, a pilgrim bottle, tin glaze in glass, a winged scarab, two Nubian finger rings, two tinned bronze bowls, and a bowl of pewter. For bronze, see pp. 174ff..

a pilgrim bottle; but tin was also employed as a glaze on glass. Other tin items in Egypt run to the Byzantine period. While in the Cairo museum we saw what is possibly an ingot of tin.

In the Eighteenth Dynasty Egypt erupted fully into the age of glass and bronze. Eaton and McKerrell's analyses of the relative proportions of arsenic and tin in Egyptian bronzes suggests that only then was Egypt moving from the phase of arsenical coppers to the phase of tin bronzes.[5]

The common theory of the Bronze Age over the past 50 years is that expressed by Alfred Lucas in his book on Egyptian materials: namely that tin bronze was a west Asian discovery, only coming late to Egypt.[4] And it seems from Eaton and McKerrell's analyses noted in *World Archaeology* that Egypt may have lagged behind Troy, Anatolia and Iran in moving from arsenical copper to tin bronze.[5]

Egyptian mirrors of the fifth and sixth dynasties evidence an advanced silvering technique based upon arsenic plating. Eaton and McKerrell make a case that the unknown metallic substance known as *d* (m) was in fact arsenical copper. They suggest, perhaps wrongly, that it was imported.

The new evidence on Egyptian tin, however, forces one to reconsider the statistics of the Bronze Age everywhere, and especially Egypt-Sudan. Even though more than 50 years of archeological finds are now represented in the bronzes analysed, the fact remains that Middle Eastern coppers and bronzes are happenstance artifacts, inadequately dated at best. One cannot and should not make a case for the discovery of bronze based on the small cassiterite deposits of Egypt. Nevertheless, given the present evidence on locations of copper, arsenic, and tin, in the Middle East, he can at least predicate a larger zone of trade and experimentation in all materials comprehending the Nile Valley and Red Sea along with the Black and Caspian Seas and the Persian Gulf.

We return to the question that has been at issue these fifty years since the study of the composition of bronzes by the Sumerian Copper Committee of the British Academy began in earnest.[6] If tin does demonstrably occur in bronzes going back to 3000 B.C. or earlier, where did the non-Egyptian tin come from? Let us move chronologically through my ten years search and the logic behind it.

Experts will have their answer to my question and will indeed challenge the old assumption that the Age of Bronze had its origins in the Eastern Mediterranean.

I shall give my reasons why I believe that the discovery of tin as a metal came in conjunction with the discovery of such other metals as arsenic, lead-silver, gold, antimony, and iron. It occurred within the frame of the great experimentation on copper-bronze that seems inevitably to have first taken place within the geographic and ecologic context of the Eastern Mediterranean, Black Sea, Caspian Sea, Persian Gulf, and Red Sea. But I shall also agree that tin in the Middle East was only an *hors d'oeuvre*; and I accept Muhly's thesis that by Mycenaean times at latest, European tin played a central role in what was left of the Bronze Age after the first incursions of iron.[7]

The five bodies of evidence that in the mid-1960's made a search for tin seem worthwhile were as follows:[8]

---

[5] See F. R. Eaton and Hugh McKerrell. 1976. "Near Eastern Alloying and Some Textual Evidence for the Early Use of Arsenical Copper." *World Archaeology* 8:2. (October, 1976), pp. 169-91.

[6] On the Sumerian Committee see H. J. Plenderleith. 1934. "Metals and Metal Technique." In C. Leonard Woolley, *Ur Excavations*, Vol. II. *The Royal Cemetery*.(Philadelphia: University of Pennsylvania Museum), pp. 289-310.

[7] J. D. Muhly. 1973. "Tin Trade Routes of the Bronze Age." *American Scientist*. 61 (July-August, 1973), pp. 403-13.

[8] For the following evidence and a bibliography see Theodore A. Wertime. 1968. "In Search of *Anaku*, Bronze-Age Mystery." *Mid-East*, 8 (May-June 1968), 11-20. Same author. 1973. "The Beginnings of Metallurgy: A New Look." *Science*, 182 (November, 1973), pp. 875-87. Same author. 1965. "Man's First Encounters With Metallurgy." *Science*, 146 (Dec. 1964),

1. The several hundred translated tablets from Kültepe and Mari containing references to trade in *anāku* from the east, suggesting an origin for tin in Elam or Iran. After the long debate over the logogram *anāku* it seemed that the trade item must concern tin rather than lead or exotic glazes or arsenical copper.

2. The reference of the geographer Strabo to tin in Drangiana, or Seistan, which tin had been exhausted.

3. The writings of the Arab geographers Muqaddasi and Mostaufi. Muqaddosi identified tin as coming from around Hamadan. Mostaufi said that tin was found in nut-sized shapes in the Lur river basin.

4. The first findings in the mid-sixties by the Geological Surveys of Iran, Afghanistan, and Turkey of trace appearances of tin. I refer to the black sands of the Caspian near the mouth of the Sefidrud; tin traces in polymetallic copper deposits in ancient Pactia south of Kabul (Mukur); and finally tin in the Arakli copper deposits near Trabizon, in Turkey. More recently, similar tin traces have been found by the Iranian Geological Survey at Chah Kalapie in Seistan.[9]

5. And, as I have indicated before, the growing evidence that bronze metallurgy and pyrotechnology developed in polymaterial settings, not where a single ore, such as tin, was abundant.

Iran

These evidences dictated my initial strategy for a reconnaissance in Iran. This was put into effect in 1967, with the help of a senior geologist of the U.S. Bureau of Mines, Abe Shekarchi. The conjunction of evidence about the old Medean-Achaemenian capital of Hamadan pointed inevitably to the pegmatites of the Alvaend range in that vicinity. The parts per million traces in the black sands of the Caspian led to a dual strategy in the basin of the Sefidrud or White River, a vast watershed extending from Tabriz on the west to nearly Qazvin on the east. Here we could sample only a few pegmatites and instead concentrated on grab samples from the subsidiary river basins.

One from this experience could say something about the techniques of panning to separate the heavy metallic sands from the lighter sands. Obviously, optimism played a role in the collection of more than a hundred carefully chosen samples from the tributaries of a great river system. At some point one expects to find a few tell-tale trains of cassiterite issuing from the vast granite basin of the Alborz, especially when traces of cassiterite had already been found at the mouth of one of the rivers. We did not see a one. The University of Minnesota, which subjected the stream samples to neutron activation analysis after our initial visual and spectroscopic investigations, discovered that it was a dry lode. It was so dry that it yielded less tin than an average granite rock anywhere.

Nothing daunted, we turned to the more promising environment of Mt. Alvaend at Hamadan, for which it seemed that the geographer Muqaddasi was the authority. In that setting the pegmatites lie directly astride

pp. 1257-67. Same author. 1968. "A Metallurgical Expedition Through the Persian Desert." *Science* 159 (March, 1968), pp. 927-35. Same author. 1976. "National Geographic Society–Smithsonian Pyrotechnological Reconnaissance of Afghanistan, Iran, and Turkey, 1968." In Paul H. Oehser, *National Geographic Society Research Reports.* (Washington: National Geographic Society), pp. 483-92.

[9]J. Stocklin, J. Eftekhar-Nezhed, and A. Hushmand-Zadeh. 1972. "Central Lut Reconnaissance, East Iran," Geological Survey of Iran. *Report No. 22,* pp. 5-60.

the famous Ganj-nameh or treasury tablets of Darius I. One is reminded of Muqaddasi by the tomb in Hamadan of his famous fellow scholar Avicenna or Ibn-Sina. Here again, we had no luck whatever, neither in the granites of Alvaend nor in the rivers of Luristan, site of the most famous bronzes in Iran. Our lack of success was matched by that of Iranian and French geologists who in the late 1960's prospected the same region in much greater depth. Where the Lurs were getting their tin was an utter mystery.

The last foray into Iran was in May of 1976, with the assistance of the Iranian Geological Survey. It must be added that only with the help of the Geological Surveys of Iran, Afghanistan, Turkey, Thailand, and Egypt, has the search for tin flourished. In this case the Iranian Geological Survey in a reconnaissance of the Eastern Dashte Lut during the early 1970's had discovered traces of tin in borings near old copper slags at Chah Kalapie. The site seemed to have some historical significance in being located northwest of the village of Neh, from which Alexander the Great plunged into Bactria; and in a general region of the Eastern Lut marked both by granites and the slags of old coppper workings. If Strabo had had any personal or even second-hand conversance with tin in Seistan it would have been at such a pivotal site.

To make a long story short, I found no current signs of workable cassiterite or stannite in the eastern desert of Iran. I do believe that the granites of this region and of adjoining Afghanistan and Pakistan and certainly India will in time yield small workable yields of tin. The copper-iron deposits at Mukur in Afghanistan have already yielded traces.

Turkey

The trail turned to Turkey in 1968 and was pursued assiduously in the years 1970, 1971, 1972, and 1976. One evidence was adventitious. In 1968, my team of pyrotechnologic reconnoiterers, which included metallurgist Ronald Tylecote and geologist Frederick Klinger, came by happenstance upon the extensive belt of black sands along the Black Sea coast of Turkey. With the memory of the analytic studies of the black sands of the Caspian fresh in hand, we were elated at first by the possibilities of cassiterite in these granite-derived sands. An additional fillip was given to our interest by the fact that C. W. Ryan's *Guide to the Known Minerals of Turkey*[10] mentioned reports of tin in a number of localities in Turkey, most prominently Balekesir.

Once again, more than five years of analytic work in Turkey carried on by the M.T.A. (Minerals Research Organization) and supplemented by assisting geologists from such organizations as the U.S. Geological Survey and the United Nations have yielded no evidences of cassiterite. The black sands proved to be high in magnetite, up to 80 percent at some river deltas. They are pregnant for the history of such iron-working peoples as the Chalybs, but not of tin or bronze. Indeed, the present Turkish government has taken the lead of the ancients and of the Ottomans in beginning to exploit them for smelting.

A hasty survey by George Rapp, James Muhly, and me in 1972 of some of the traditional sites, such as Balekesir, reinforced the conclusion of Turkish geologists that no known cassiterite exists in Turkey. Again, in May of 1976, I searched the fluorites of Sivas for some traces of stannite, but without benefit of the expert who claims that stannite is there. The occasional analytic traces of stannite in Turkish copper deposits, such as Arakli, persuade one that Turkey may indeed have stannite which passes unrecognized by its geologists.

---

[10] Published by United States Operations Mission to Turkey in December, 1957.

Greece

The rumor of tin in Greece has long been scotched by geologists and mining companies. I personally have checked out reported possibilities at Itea near Delphi and in the famous black sands of Santorini. Rapp and Muhly have been equally alert to any putative evidences in Greece.

Our major foray into early Minoan-Mycenaean bronze metallurgy in Greece took place in 1973 at John Caskey's site of Ayia Irini on the island of Kea. Tylecote, Muhly, Vincent Pigott, and I spent several weeks in a review of the numerous crucibles at that site and were persuaded that oxhide copper ingots from the eastern Mediterranean were being wedded to foreign tin in the crucibles of Kea. But as is usual at archeological sites, there had been not a clue as to tin sources. This was before the finds of two Cypro-Minoan bars of tin off Israel during the summer of 1976. These ingots are now undergoing analysis.

Thailand

Since the late 1960's, under the respective influences of Colin Renfrew and Wilhelm Solheim there has been a recrudescence of interest in the major deposits of tin in both Europe and Thailand-Malaysia as possible points of origins of the art of making bronze. These possibilities have been followed up by Chester Gorman in his dig at Ban Chiang[11] in Thailand and Hugh McKerrell in his analyses of Eurasian and Egyptian bronzes. Because of Gorman's spectacular finds of bronzes in Thailand dated as early as 3600 B.C. by radiocarbon, George Rapp and I visited Ban Chiang in 1974. One is overwhelmed by the amount of tin present in Thailand as cassiterite or wood tin and by the exploited possibilities of experimentation with tin *qua* tin.

Historically there is much use of the pure metal. There is even iron dated 1600-1400 B.C.. One obviously must tread with care in such an area, especially when it is now claimed that Thailand gave the invention of bronze to both Southwestern Asia and China.

My own doubts remain simply because one does not yet find in Thailand an infrastructure of developing copper and gold metallurgy, or of polymetallism sufficient to explain the first exploitation of either tin or bronze. This may appear in time under the careful nurturing of Solheim and Gorman. One sees no evidence in the Persian Gulf that the tin of Thailand was ever traded to Sumer or the west; I have personally queried Geoffrey Bibby re traces of tin in the sands of Dilmun. Nor are there evidences that Thais or Cornishmen were dancing attendance in any way on the first makers of bronze in the eastern Mediterranean.

Egypt - Sudan

The recent reconnaissance of Egypt reinforces the impression of an independent origin of bronze in the Middle East as does the consistent record of tin artifacts and glazes from the 18th dynasty (1580 B.C.) onward. After the long drought it was most refreshing to move up three wadis of the Eastern Desert of Egypt and see the trail of cassiterite as the first prospectors must have found it. These wadis were in the lee of mines at Igla, Nuweibi, and El-Mueilha, all within a radius of 150 km. from Marsa Alam in the Red Sea. In each, the torrential rains that fall every 5-10 years had dislodged the grains of black cassiterite, leaving a sparking trail in every riffle capable of catching the heavier grains of SnO_2. The same phenomena marked the Sabaloka mines on the sixth cataract of the Nile, near a major archeological source of bronze in Nubia.

---

[11]Chester Gorman and Pisit Charoenwongsa. 1976. "Ban Chiang: A Mosaic of Impressions From the First Two Years." *Expedition*, 18 (Summer 1976), pp. 14-26.

How do we move beyond the presumption from the earliest tin bronzes and glazes of Egypt that such wadis were anciently exploited? Igla, for example, was last mined during the dire shortages of tin of World War II; one can still see the smelter and the glassy glazes of tin and slags at the site. Was this the earliest working?

One derives little comfort from the oral tradition of the Bedouins, who have located most of the ancient workings and significant contemporary ore deposits of Egypt for the Geological Survey and Mining Authority of Egypt. Their terms are *shokle qadimi* or *shokle Romani*, meaning ancient or Roman works. Only in Nubia or the Sudan is the term *shokle pharaoni* in use, explicitly referring to the pharaonic period. In this respect the traditions differ not a whit from those of Iran where the Assyrian Shaeddad (Assurbanipal?) is evoked for early metals; or Cyprus and Spain where the chief burgeoning of metals is dated to the Phoenicians and Romans.

More promising are two indications of pharaonic dates driven home to us in Egypt.

1. The fact that the tin-bearing greisens or muscovites are extensions of gold-bearing quartz veins, and that the sweeping search for gold evidently led men to speculate about minerals found in conjunction with gold. The earliest known reference to gold appears to date to the reign of Menes, first historical ruler of Egypt, though gold-handled daggers of stone date to the Predynastic period.[12] The earliest inscriptions in the mines and quarries of the Wadi Hammamat date from the fifth and sixth dynasties. The written record in the twelfth dynasty referred to the gold mines of the Hammamat. In Saqqara tombs dating ca. 2400 B.C. one has a depiction of gold workers melting the gold with blowpipes. The pharaoh Chephren, builder of one of the great pyramids of Giza, had several statues of himself made of anorthosite, found in conjunction with gold-bearing veins. There was much alluvial gold, which would also have brought prospectors directly into contact with the stream tin. At Nuweibi tin mines we found a grinder similar to the ancient grinders for gold.

2. The presence near the El-Mueilha tin mines of possibly eight inscriptions, identifying this as the spot to which Pharaoh Pepi II (22nd c. B.C.) sent men for "stone" (hardly for the second-rate granites around the site).

One thus finds in Egypt and Nubia a marvelous integration of metallurgy and pyrotechnology centering about gold and later bronze and glass and ultimately yielding a consistent record of artifacts and glazes of tin. The drought in ancient tin sources in the Eastern Mediterranean is at last broken, thanks to the Egyptian Geological Survey, but broken not through a consistent rainfall but a single deluge per decade such as brings out the stream cassiterite at Nuweibi. I reiterate: we are only at the end of the beginning. Where does one turn next?

There undoubtedly are other tin mines in Egypt-Nubia contributing not a little to the slowly evolving bronze age in those countries. Yet no evidence exists to suggest that Egyptian tin was a trade item as were gold and copper. One remains, therefore, in the dark concerning tin for the bronze age, as elsewhere in the old Middle East.

---

[12]Stanley C. Dunn. 1911. "Ancient Gold Mining in the Sudan." Fourth Report of the Wellstone Tropical Research Laboratories at the Gordon Memorial College, Khartoum. Vol. 2. *Geological Science.* W. F. Hume, *Geology of Egypt,* Vol. II, 699ff.. Hume carries numerous illustrations of the gold of ancient Egypt.

The Garden of Ancient Egypt

by

Leslie Mesnick Gallery
Architect and Landscape Designer, Philadelphia

The customary images of Egyptian civilization are the architectural monuments set in splendid isolation in the dry, barren, monochromatic desert. The present settings of the ruins contain few reminders of the landscape which actually surrounded them—a lush green "oasis"—or the gardens which existed within them.

For the Egyptians the total composition of the temples and palaces consisted of an interplay between architecture and landscape. Even in a complex such as the great pyramids of Giza the fundamental architectural forms imply a landscape; the simple pyramidal form can symbolize an eternal mountain, or be interpreted as an abstract image of mountain in the same way as the conical rocks of a Japanese dry garden symbolize landscape (Ills. 1 & 2). The pyramids are seen in isolation which emphasizes the vastness of the pyramid as an element in the landscape, equating the pyramidal form with the natural form of a mountain. The conical elements and the pyramidal forms in their settings are viewed as one landscape composition, rather than as a series of separate elements. This is representative of an attitude which places architecture as a complementary part of the landscape.

While the pyramids are an abstract landscape form, Deir el Bahari is integrated more directly into its landscape. The site is sober and monotonous, with a wall of mountains as the horizon. The face of these cliffs changes in response to the movement of the sun. Deir el Bahari is related to these cliffs by three terraces which rise from the valley floor, and by the colonnade which echoes the modulation of the cliffs in the contrasting light and dark of columns and voids.

This love of nature, expressed in the relationship between architecture and its setting, is seen in architecture in the use of natural motifs as architectural elements, and in the interweaving of inside-outside space as the dwelling sits in the garden, a simple formal architectural complex.

In Egyptian architecture natural forms, used for the columns and capitals, preserve the flora of ancient Egypt, and represent an inventory of the vegetation. The images most frequently used were those of the palm, lily, papyrus, and lotus. The capitals at the temple of Amon at Luxor, for example are in the form of a lotus bundle (bundle lotiform) (Ill. 3), and those at the temple of Tutmoses III are a bundle of opening buds of the fragile lotus. The palm leaf capital seen at Abusir refers to the date palm forests. In addition to expressing a profound interest in nature, the use of natural forms as architectural elements is symbolic of geographical areas of Egypt. The combined use of plant forms from the north and the south in one structure represents the unity of southern and northern Egypt. An open papyriform with triangular stem which imitates a single shaft of papyrus such as seen in a column from the complex of Zoser symbolizes Lower Egypt (Ill. 4); while the lily capital, represented by curving sides in the shape of volutes, is symbolic of Upper Egypt. At times more than one plant form was represented, as seen in the composite capital (Ill. 5).

While the influence of nature was expressed architecturally in the relationship between the buildings and their sites, and in the frequent use of plant forms as architectural elements, the Egyptians' reverence for nature becomes very apparent when studying their gods, the importance of trees in worship, and the place of the garden in the life after death.

The representation of the god of gardens, Khem, offers further evidence of the importance of nature in the life of the Egyptian. Khem was the god who presided over the garden. Khem was also the god of generation. As the god of generation, Khem was responsible for the procreation and continuation of species. In representations of Khem symbolic trees are found behind the deity (Ill. 6). The same image of "tree" used in representations of Khem is seen in the hieroglyphic group which contains a tree and a sign of the land meaning Egypt (Ill. 7). Thus, this grouping bears an evident relation to the deity Khem. The name Khem is similar to the word Chenoa, by which Egypt was known in Coptic. The hieroglyphics on the rosetta stone which imply Egypt are read as the land of trees.

The stylized image most often used as the symbol of tree in ancient Egyptian art was probably the sycamore (ficus sycamorous), also known as the wild fig (Nehet). Untrained, this tree had a heavy gnarled trunk with low masses of compact foliage which created a dense shade on the edge of the desert. At times the leaves of this tree were trained in a formal manner. Because the sycamore tree was so popular in the Egyptian garden its formalized image was used to symbolize all trees.

The Egyptians loved trees not only for their intrinsic beauty but for their cooling shade. Further indication of the reverence with which people treated trees is shown in a tomb painting which portrays a peasant worshipping the sycamore tree by bringing it offerings.

Another example of the importance of the tree is seen in the scene of a god painting Ramese's II name on yshit tree at Thebes (Ill. 8). This is the tree of history on which the gods depict the name and deeds of the pharaoh.

Since the Egyptians believed in a life after death, a small garden was often created in front of the tomb so the soul could enjoy the pleasures of his garden in the next world as he had in this one (Ill. 9). Another way of representing this devotion is seen in the representation of the tomb of Osiris with sacred tamarisk (Ill. 10). This is a symbolic picture of a garden in the form of a bird, Bennu. Here Osiris sits on the sacred tamarisk tree at the entrance to the tomb.

Gardens were also painted on the walls of the death chamber, as seen in the "Festival of the dead in the garden of Rekhmara" (Ill. 11). The scene shows the dead man taking leave of his possessions as he is rowed over a pool of water by his servants, a part of a special death feast held in his garden. The dead man's actual garden is represented here. A similar scene from the Old Kingdom showed the garden to be very formal (Ill. 12). This primitive garden of the dead from the Old Kingdom was composed of a geometric tank of water with an uneven number of palms on either side. An inscription from the tomb of Apoui at Thebes reinforces the love of the garden which the scenes from the tomb paintings portrayed:

> That each day I may walk unceasingly on the banks of my water, that my
> soul may repose on the branches of the trees which I planted, that I may
> refresh myself under the shadow of my sycamore.[1]

The importance of nature in Egyptian life was illustrated most clearly in the emphasis placed on the garden —its major role in their daily life and its importance in the total estate complex. One of the more important contributions from the Egyptian garden is this emphasis on outdoor living. The total estate, consisting of

---

[1]Gotheim, Marie, *A History of Garden Art,* Vol. I, E. P. Dutton & Company, New York, 1928.

house and garden, was enclosed by a wall. Its composition was very architectural in form. The major portion of the walled-in estate, however, was garden while only a minor portion was house. Clearly the primary living space in the estate complex was the outdoor area of the garden. While the garden takes its language from the vocabulary of architectural form it is the garden, not the house, which is dominant.

The basic elements of the Egyptian garden are most clearly illustrated in the reconstructed drawing of the estate of a high official during the reign of Amenhotep III at Thebes (Ills. 13 & 14). The garden was enclosed by a wall, and composed in rectilinear order. The garden contained geometric pools of water and a large pergola. To enter the estate one passed by a large canal which was connected to the river and used as a source of irrigation. Between the canal and wall of the complex a row of trees, probably sycamores, shaded the wall. The complex was entered by passing through a main gate directly into the garden.

This large garden was divided into different parts. First, one stepped into a little vineyard. As one walked to the main house, the vineyards provided not only grapes, but shade. This vineyard was constructed from transverse rafters which rested on pillars. Vines were trained on a trellis supported by rafters; a wall surrounded the vineyard, defining it as a major element in the garden. Outside the vineyard were rows of palm trees.

The remainder of the garden was divided into rectilinear areas by low walls and walks. There were four tanks of water. These rectangular tanks, each bordered by a grassy plot with papyrus growing in clumps nearby, was filled with geese, fish, water lilies, and lotus. These ponds were primarily used for irrigation, but also provided a source of food, as well as pleasure.

Each section within the garden was enclosed by a low wall. The reconstruction shows a small subdivision between the large and small pond which is interpreted as a special grove or orchard due to its complete enclosure. In the center of the garden was a three story house; smaller summer houses or porch-like pavillions appear near the water.

Thus in this strictly formal and architectural garden are the elements of the modern garden: the wall, originally needed for protection from sand storms and roaming animals; the pool, once needed for irrigation; the geometric layout of beds, always the most efficient method of planting and caring for vegetation; and the pergola, which originated as a vineyard and provided shade. Within the garden landscape elements of great variety were used primarily for utilitarian purposes. Alternating along the peripheral wall of the estate of a high official at Thebes were the doum palm, date palm, and sycamore.

By the time of the New Kingdom, exotic plants, including the almond tree, apple tree, jasmine, and myrrh were known; however, the doum palm remained one of the most important trees in the life of the ancient Egyptian. The doum palm or Thebean palm (crucifera thebaica) was primarily grown south of Thebes.[2] Coconut came from this palm. The fruit, called gûgû, was a large round nut often used to make drills. The doum palm was readily recognizable by its form. It bifurcated or split at eight to ten yards above the ground. The branches divided and terminated in bunches of 20-30 palmates with fibrous leaves six to eight feet long. This tree produced very solid wood which was often used for rafts.

Among the more important trees found in the Egyptian garden was the date palm (phoenix dactylifera). The trunk, which rose uninterrupted to a height of 13-16 yeards, was used for beams; its branches were used for wicker baskets, and its leaves for mats and brooms. The date palm could be grown from cuttings and live to 60 or 70 years. Each August the dates were gathered in preparation for either being preserved as a

---

[2]Also referred to as Hyphaene thebatica.

jam or dried. This tree was most popular for its fruit. Its tall slender form topped by a crown of 2-3 tiers of flexible leaves did not, however, keep out the sun (Ill. 15).

In addition to the trees mentioned earlier a number of others were found in residential gardens. The tamarisk (tamarix gallica) was very common;[3] it yielded a food called manna. The leaves of the willows (salix or tarit), were used for funeral garlands during the 18th or 20th Dynasties.

The fruit and wood of the lotus zizyphus, or Bubsu, was often found in tombs.

Strychnus, a genus of tropical trees and woody vines, was also evident in the Egyptian flora. Strychnus was a valuable drug, from which poison was made.

The tomb paintings, showing the monkeys picking the fruit of the fig tree, give evidence of the ficus carica within the garden complex (Ill. 16).

In the 18th Dynasty the pomegranate was introduced and was found in the gardens of Tutmoses III (Ill. 17). Other fruit trees recorded in the Egyptian gardens were the olive (introduced in the New Kingdom), almond tree, peach tree, bay tree and caster berry tree. The persea (persea gratissma) or avocado was often considered to be sacred.

The carob tree (ceratonia siliqua) provided shade with its dense glossy evergreen leaves and was frequently used for avenue planting.[4]

We are all familiar with the lotus which is portrayed regularly in the tomb paintings. There was the white lotus (nymphaea lotus) and the blue lotus (nymphaea coerulea). These were used in wreaths, as table decorations, and as ornament in women's hair.

Some illustrations include a bell-shaped plant. This plant appears to be from the convolvulaceae family which includes morning glory and bindweed.

Papyrus grew in dense clumps in Northern Egypt. Its stems, which often reach six times the height of a man, provided a resting place for birds.

Although the gardens were primarily utilitarian, flowers were also found in the ancient Egyptian garden. Among the flowers found in the gardens were the chrysanthemum and anemone. The frequent portrayal of flowers and wild life scenes continues to reinforce the evidence of the Egyptian love for nature. Flowers were often used as a decorative element in tomb paintings, such as in the painting which depicts Amenhotep IV in a pond with flower beds, or as a floral motif on the palace floor from Amarna (Ill. 18).

A fondness for flowers, reflected by abundant daily use, was present in the life of the Egyptians. They were used as an offering when greeting guests, or as offering to the master of the house (Ill. 19). The flowers from the garden were also used as garlands, bouquets, table decoration and in wreaths to symbolize rebirth.

While the plan of an estate of a high official at Thebes illustrates the layout of the garden, the tomb, painting expresses the Egyptian attitudes toward the role of the garden in the Egyptian's life after death as seen in a painting of a garden from a villa at Thebes (Ill. 20). This shows visitors being entertained in the garden, under the shade of an outdoor porch. The house, shown inside the garden, again was enclosed entirely by a wall. The entrance gate always led directly into the garden through which one then proceeded

---

[3]There is a discrepancy as to whether this was a tamarix gallica or tamarix nilotica.

[4]This tree is often referred to as a locust tree because the seeds and pulp from it were supposedly the locust and wild honey which St. John ate in the wilderness.

to the house. In this example the garden was shown going all around the house, as represented by the trees behind the house. The most conspicuous place in the complex was reserved for the arbour.

From these examples a picture of the typical garden emerges. The garden was divided into vegetables, flowers, vineyards and orchards. Usually each section was separate within the total enclosure, but occasionally the vineyard and arbour were not separated from each other and were continuous. Rows of columns supported rafters which divided the vineyard into numerous avenues. The trellis style was efficient as it intercepted rays of sun and allowed greater moisture to be maintained at the roots. The earlier trellises were supported by a simple forked pillar (Ill. 21). A later development was the more refined round vine arbour (Ill. 22). The capitals on pillars which supported the structure of the trellis eventually became very elaborate, and vines were then trained in decorative ways (Ill. 23). The building which housed the wine press was frequently situated within the area of the vineyard.

Perhaps one of the main determinants of the form of the Egyptian garden was the availability of water. Because of the scarcity of water, all gardens were designed to use the minimum amount of water most efficiently. A great deal of thought and concern went into the development of watering devices (Ills. 24 & 25). One such device was a shadūf or well sweep. This device, still used in Egypt today, was used to bring water from the lower ground to the higher by placing a bucket on one end of a pole and a weight on the other.

The water was then carried through a narrow open channel into the garden, inside the garden the channel might widen, to form a rectangular pool. The T-shape, which served as irrigation channel and pool, was frequently surrounded by sycamores, figs, and pomegranates.

Because of the dry harsh climate a great deal of care was required to maintain the vegetation; therefore, as a result of the scarcity of water and the amount of time required to maintain these gardens, their primary importance was utilitarian. For convenience and easy maintenance the plants were arranged in individual beds with one kind of plant per bed. This arrangement is illustrated in a scene of vegetable gardens from the tomb of Beni Hassan (Ill. 26).

Vegetables usually found in the garden included garlic, onions, leeks, lupine, beans, chick peas, melonkhia (like endive), and arum colocasia (a root cooked in water).

It was also quite common to find trees planted in pots for easier maintenance. The process of planting small trees in pots was developed by Ramses II (Ill. 27). He was a great lover of plants, and introduced many plants into Egypt, planted trees in new towns, created great vineyards, and imported flowers from all countries.

While the gardens of the upper class citizens were well developed, those of the priestly class were even larger (Ills. 28 & 29). The residence and garden of a high priest at Tel el Amarna (also known as the palace of Merire) during the reign of King Amenhotep IV was actually a completely walled-in working farm and as such, comparable to the farm estates (villa rustica) of Roman civilization. The estate maintained the basic characteristics of the Egyptian garden. It was walled-in, and arranged geometrically. There was a gate on either side of the main entrance. Once inside one approached a walk shaded by rows of trees. Facing the door of the right and left wing were two spacious water tanks. Between the two wings of the house was an avenue of trees which led to the stable. In one wing was an open court, entered after passing through an outer door. The court was planted with trees which extended around the nucleus of the inner apartment. In the back of the wing was the entrance to a smaller garden. Within this garden was a small summer house, and in the center of this walled-in section was a large tank of water with stairs in the corner of the pool.

A variety of trees were contained in this smaller garden. Trees were commonly planted in individual beds of saucer-like formations with a rim around the perimeter. The rim sloped inward toward the base of the tree in order to preserve the water (Ill. 30). An irrigation channel can be seen in the plan.

This villa, which was similar to a small farm, included within its walls a granary, a stable for horses, a shelter and feeding area for cattle. The farmyard in which the cattle were kept was farthest from the house.

Eventually each section of this farm-like garden/estate was given a specific name such as vineyard, orchard, kitchen and flower garden. Later a large park was added to the gardens of the rich. This park served as a game preserve for a hunt.

These gardens, which were grand gardens belonging to the wealthy and the royalty, were primarily outside of the city; but garden living and the love of nature were so much a part of the culture and of the residential dwelling, that we can see, even in smaller residential dwellings, an emphasis and a concern for the relationship between the inside space and the courtyard (Ills. 31 & 32).

On another scale, the Egyptian temple was the center for the development of horticulture, advances in garden design and experimentation with new plants. Each temple park had a grove of trees. Although the main purpose of these trees was religious, they were also planted for shade revenue, and scientific study. In these temple gardens exotic trees were particularly valued and held sacred. An example of a reconstruction of a temple shows it to be completely surrounded by the temenos, or grove (Ill. 33). A procession with a sacred boat advances. Occasionally a wooden model of the grove was carried in the procession. In the procession the trees were carried behind the god Khem.

As there were no major natural green areas, the gardens of the temples became the predominant areas in which greenery was found. These green estates began to form a linear pattern of irrigated agricultural land along the Nile.

Perhaps the best known example of an Egyptian temple is found at Deir el Bahari (c. 1500 B.C.). Today it is seen as a barren architectural monument (Ill. 34). During the time of Queen Hatshepsut it was a green oasis in the desert, with trees planted on each of the three terraces and acacias lining the entrance.[5]

Once inside the gates there was a luxurious garden filled with trees, imported from the land of Punt,[6] carried aboard a ship. Their roots were dug in earthern balls, and then packed in baskets, later to be transported in baskets hung from supports on the shoulders of slaves (Ill. 35). Thrity-two incense bearing trees were planted in large holes in the rocks, holes filled with rich and fertile Nile mud. They thrived in their new home. The illustration shows the trees having grown large enough for cattle to graze underneath their branches (Ill. 36).

Deir el Bahari is a good example of the limitations of looking at the ruins of the palaces, temples, and tombs as they exist today, for at the time of their construction they were as dependent on landscape as on architecture. The desert-like temple complex we see today conveys little of the feeling which must have existed during the reign of Queen Hatshepsut. The complex needs the trees to complete the true image of the monumental temple.

Throughout the history of ancient Egypt, and its architecture, the landscape was vital to the image of the total design. The formally planted landscape, at times lush and green, was highly developed and fundamental to the total picture of the building, both at the scale of the residential dwelling, and the temple complex (Ill. 37).

---

[5]Four varieties of acacias were found at this time: acacia nilotica (mimosa), known as SONT; acacia seyel (myrtle) which was used as a source of wood for carpenters; acacia abbida on which grew a white flower; and acacia farnesiana which has fragrant feathery branches of yellow flowers.

[6]Egyptian name for part of Africa not certainly identified.

References

Most of the facts on which this article is based are from Wilkinson (1842), Gotheim (1928), Maspero (1901).

Primary Bibliography

ADOLPH, ERMAN
  1969   *Life in Ancient Egypt.* New York: Benjamin Blom.
BADAWI, ALEXANDER
  1966   *Architecture in Ancient Egypt and the Near East.* Cambridge, Massachusetts: M.I.T. Press.
GOTHEIM, MARIE
  1928   *A History of Garden Art,* Vol. I. New York: E. P. Dutton and Company.
HYAMS, EDWARD
  1971   *A History of Gardens and Gardening.* New York: Praeger.
MASPERO, G. C. R.
  1901   *The Dawn of Civilization.* London: Society of Promoting Christian Knowledge.
MURRY, MARGARET
  1949   *The Splendor That Was Egypt.* London: Sidgwick and Jackson Ltd..
NAVILLE, EDWARD HENRI
1894-1908 *The Temple of Dier-El-Bakhari.* London: Office of Egyptian Exploration Fund.
WILKINSON, J. GARDNER
1837-1841 *Manners and Customs of the Ancient Egyptians.*
  1842   *A Popular Account of the Ancient Egyptians.* London: John Murray.

Additional Bibliography

"Aus alten Ägyptischen Garten von Landschafts – Architekt Eryk Pepinski." In *Wasmuths Monatshefte für Baukunst,* V.A. 9, pp. 441-43, 1925.
EIBL, ANTON
  1938   "Ägyptische Privatgarten, eine kunstgeschichtliche Betrachtung." *Garten Kunst* 51:25-29.
HARTMANN, F.
  1923   *L'agriculture dans l'ancienne Egypte.* Paris.
JELLICOE, GEOFFREY and SUSAN
  1975   *The Landscape of Man.* New York: Viking Press.
KEIMER, L.
  1924   *Die Gardenpflanzen im alten Ägypten.,* 2 vols. Hamburg.
PERRET, ANTOINETTE
  1935   "History of the Country Estate." *Country Life* 68, September.
PETRIE, FLINDERS, W. M.
  1910   *Arts and Crafts of Ancient Egypt.* Chicago: A. C. McClurg.
THOMPSON, DOROTHY BURR
  1950   "Parks and Gardens of The Ancient Empires." *Archaeology* 3, 2:101-06.
WOENIG, F.
  1897   *Die Pflanzen im Alten Aegypten.* Leipzig.

Tradition and Revolution
in the Art of the XVIIIth Dynasty

by

Cyril Aldred
The Royal Scottish Museum, Edinburgh, Great Britain

It has become a commonplace that the art of the XVIIIth Dynasty in Ancient Egypt reverted to the inspiration of the early Middle Kingdom style as a point of departure and thereafter went its own way.[1] Indeed, the evidence for this at Thebes is rather compelling. The reliefs of Amosis from Abydos and Karnak,[2] and those of Amenophis I at Karnak[3] show in their iconography and the character of their inscriptions a departure from the design of the monuments of Kamose and his immediate predecessors[4], and a return to the style which prevailed during the late XIth and early XIIth Dynasties.

The stela of Amosis from Abydos[5] recalls the work of Nebhepetre from Tod[6] closely in its style and proportions (Ills. 1 and 2). The reliefs of Amenophis I in the alabaster shrine from the Third Pylon at Karnak,[7] and the fragment in Brooklyn[8] take their inspiration from the monuments of S'ankhkare at Tod and Armant.[9] Only the inscriptions and the details of dress, such as the king's Blue Crown and the queen's sceptre distinguish the work of the later from that of the earlier period.

There were good reasons why the Theban craftsmen should have reverted to the examples of an earlier age for their inspiration. The re-establishing of a unified Egyptian state in the XVIIIth Dynasty had been the work of the aggressive Thebans under the vigorous leadership of their princes. The patriotism that was aroused in the peoples of Upper Egypt by the so-called war of liberation against their Hyksos overlords found expression also in the local pride of the Theban craftsmen, who in seeking to re-establish the highest standards, looked naturally to their own past achievements for guidance. Monuments of the Mentuhoteps and Sesostris I at Armant, Karnak, Tod, Medamud and Western Thebes were still standing, virtually intact, as classic examples of splendid works commissioned by the illustrious and deified ancestors of the Theban line. As late as the early reign of Tuthmosis III the funerary temple of Nebhepetre at Deir el-Bahri could provide a challenge and an inspiration to the architect of Hatshepsut's great monument on the same site, though the first tentative imitation was soon replaced with a more ambitious and grander conception as the building progressed.[10]

---

[1] Hayes (1959) p. 43; Smith (1965) p. 128; Redford (1967) p. 78.

[2] James (1965) p. 18; Porter & Moss (1927-74) II, rev. edn. p. 73.

[3] *Ibid.* pp. 63-64.

[4] James (1965) p. 18.

[5] Lacau (1909) No. 34002.

[6] Bisson de la Roque (1937) figs. 25-30, pls. XVII-XIX (Cairo Museum J. E. No. 66329-31).

[7] Porter & Moss (1927-74) II, rev. edn. pp. 63-64.

[8] Fazzini (1975) No. 48.

[9] Bisson de la Roque (1937) figs. 32-50, pl. XXV (Cairo Museum J. E. No. 66333-7); Mond-Myers (1940) pp. 21-22.

It is not only the royal monuments that betray the influence of Middle Kingdom archetypes. The private statuary of the period in its predilection for the figure wrapped in a cloak and either seated or squatting, maintained the volumetric qualities of the Middle Kingdom style, as in the statues of Ahmose-Ruru at Brooklyn,[11] Senmut in Berlin and Cairo[12] and Sennefer in London.[13] They differ only in showing the bland features of their owners cast in the mould of the contemporary king, Tuthmosis III, and have little of the introspection of their Middle Kingdom counterparts.

In assessing this debt to Middle Kingdom inspiration, however, it should not be forgotten that our knowledge of the art of the early XVIIIth Dynasty comes from the monuments found at Thebes. The vanished contemporary world of Lower Egypt is almost totally unknown to us, and we can perceive only darkly the influence of the metropolitan style of Memphis, which since the Archaic Period had engendered and sustained the highest traditions of Pharaonic art. But the overthrow of the last Hyksos ruler by Amosis necessarily ensured that the Theban princes fell heirs to the resources, officials, traditions and perhaps even the harim of a dynasty, which whatever the successful rebels in Thebes may have thought of it, was always regarded in Lower Egypt as a line of legitimate pharaohs. We can see that the influence of the more cosmopolitan and sophisticated culture of Lower Egypt increases as the XVIIIth Dynasty wears on, and is particularly evident in the field of religion or ideology.

A beginning is perhaps indicated by the founding at Memphis of a vast palace complex by Tuthmosis I which was still flourishing at the end of the dynasty. It was in the reign of this same king that limestone slabs sketched with a draft of the Book of Imy Duat were evidently prepared as a lining for the burial chamber of his tomb.[14] This is the first of those editions of the sacred books which under the influence of the revived solar cult of Heliopolis were to decorate the royal hypogea and their burial furniture at Thebes.[15]

There is other evidence of the impact of this same sun religion on the architecture of the Dynasty. The temple of Hatshepsut at Deir el-Bahri adds two of the colonnaded courts in which the sun-cult was observed, to the hypostyle hall and shrine of the upper terrace, essential features both of the primal temple of Egyptian Creation.[16] From thence onwards most Egyptian temples were to have such a colonnaded court or courts with the twin towers of the pylon added as a visible testimony of the solarization of Egyptian regional cults.[17] The steady growth in the authority of Heliopolitan sun-worship was to culminate in the monotheistic sun-religion of Akhenaten near the end of the Dynasty; but the antiquarian aspects of this Lower Egyptian influence have scarcely been mentioned by historians, and it is perhaps time that the balance was in some measure redressed.

In the first place, the political situation in the XVIIIth Dynasty was nearer to that which had prevailed during the early Old Kingdom. The Pharaoh was no longer the feudal lord, *primus inter pares,* which had been his fate after the end of the VIth Dynasty.[18] He was now a Homeric champion, a victorious warlord, the incarnation of such warrior gods as Baal or Mont.[19] He had attained the same lonely pre-eminence as the

---

[10]Smith (1965) pp. 128-29.

[11]Fazzini (1975) No. 49.

[12]Vandier (1952-69) III, pls. CLI, 1; CLXII, 2; Aldred (1961) No. 32.

[13]Aldred (1961) No. 48.

[14]Porter & Moss (1927-74) I, rev. edn. pt. 2, p. 557.

[15]Piankoff (1964) pp. 121ff.

[16]Reymond (1969) Ch. 13.

[17]Derchain (1966) pp. 17ff.

[18]Hayes (1961) pt. 1, pp. 7, 21, 35.

[19]Hayes (1961) pt. 2, pp. 3-5.

divine kings of the IVth Dynasty who had built their gigantic monuments at Dahshur and Gizeh. He ruled Egypt unchallenged with a similar centralized authority, though it was now a military caste rather than a technocratic élite. The tombs of his high officials were clustered on the hills of Western Thebes in sight of his mortuary temple, just as the burials of the ruling class in the IVth Dynasty were huddled around the pyramids of their lords. Not the least of the privileges that Akhenaten promised his followers was the assurance that they should have their tombs near his in the new residence-city of Akhetaten.

The impact of these ideas on the art of the period becomes more evident as the Dynasty progresses. The reliefs with which Hatshepsut decorated the walls of her mortuary temple at Deir el-Bahri appear to be inspired in their proportions and style by the reliefs from the pyramid complex of Phiops II at Sakkarah, the last great utterance of the legendary pharaohs of a classical past. This stylistic influence is particularly striking in the processions of offering-bearers in the Southern Hall of Offerings[20] (Ills. 3 and 4). It would be a matter of some delicacy, however, to decide whether this inspiration came to Hatshepsut's craftsmen direct, or through the intermediary of Middle Kingdom versions of the style of Dynasty VI.[21] Nevertheless the writer is tempted to postulate direct influence for reasons which will shortly become clearer.

In other scenes at Deir el-Bahri, the contemporary dress and accoutrements tend to give an entirely up-to-date rendering of the subjects for illustration. But it is surely permissible to wonder whether the subjects have not been selected for their traditional significance. To us they appear new because they are isolated in that context of Egyptian art which has survived to our own day. Such themes as the netting of birds, or the Pharaoh as sphinx trampling the nations underfoot which exist in a greatly damaged state in the lowermost colonnade are traditional in iconography, and congeners can be found on the shattered remains of Old Kingdom monuments.[22] On the other hand such scenes as the voyage to Punt and the transportation of the obelisks, appear to be unique since we lack any earlier examples. Yet isolated fragments of relief that have survived from the causeway of the pyramid of Wenis, show such cognate themes as the transportation of monolithic granite columns, and the arrival of Asiatics aboard ship, raising their hands in wonderment and praise.[23]

Such themes may have suggested the subjects of the Hatshepsut reliefs, if not their exact design. The expedition to Punt in the reign of the queen repeated the exploits that had been made during the Vth Dynasty, for example, in the reigns of Sahure and Isesi; and it is surely not overbold to postulate that such subjects may well have been illustrated in the lost causeway reliefs of those kings, and given inspiration to Hatshepsut's artists, whether direct or through Middle Kingdom re-interpretations. The scenes of the divine birth of Hatshepsut, too, though they were copied in the main by subsequent monarchs such as Amenophis III at Luxor and Nectanebo I at Dendereh, are not likely to have been the first of their kind. They may have had their genesis in the lost reliefs in the sun-temples of the Old Kingdom, though the earliest survival of the legend dates to the XIIth Dynasty.[24]

It may be objected that all this is really very tenuous; and perhaps it is specious to compare scenes at Deir el-Bahri with conjectural Old Kingdom reliefs which in any case have not survived. Let us at any rate admit that the XVIIIth Dynasty showed a keen and persisting interest in the monuments of the Old Kingdom. The representation of the *per wer* on the facade of the inner chambers of the Hathor shrine at Deir el-Bahri, for instance, is usually taken to be derived from a traditional design of which early examples are to be seen in the chapels on the western side of the Jubilee Court of the Step Pyramid of Djoser.[25] Evidently no one has

---

[20]Naville (1894-1908) IV, pls. CVII-CXII; Jéquier (1936-40) II, pp. 26-27; Smith (1965) p. 134.

[21]Smith (1965) p. 95, pl. 64a.

[22]Naville (1894-1908) VI, pls. CLX, CLXIII; Borchardt (1910-13) II, pl. 8.

[23]Hassan (1955) p. 137, fig. 1; *cf.* Borchardt (1910-13) II, pls. 12, 13, fig. 12, p. 134.

[24]Redford (1967) p. 83, n. 130.

[25]Borchardt (1938) pp. 23-28, pl. 10; Naville (1894-1908) IV, p. 5, pl. CIII.

considered whether the Hatshepsut version may not be a direct copy of the Djoser archetype: yet the special reverence which was shown for the great achievements of Djoser's architect, Imhotep, from this point onwards in Egyptian history, had already been paid by visitors in the reign of Amenophis I.[26]   Other graffiti disclose that scribes were making such pilgrimages in the reign of Hatshepsut[27] who boasts that she restored monuments in Middle Egypt which had stood in ruins since the Hyksos wars.[28]   This rehabilitation, doubtless in Lower as well as Middle Egypt, presupposes that careful surveys of all the standing monuments were made as a necessary preliminary to any re-building schemes.

The officials of her co-regent and successor Tuthmosis III reveal the same concern for the monuments of the Old Kingdom.   The First Herald Amunedjeh left a scribble in the sun-temple of Weserkaf, the first king of the Vth Dynasty, showing that he had inspected that monument.[29]

Another scribe in this same reign wrote in praise of King Sneferu of the IVth Dynasty on the walls of the mortuary temple of the pyramid of Meydum,[30] where the scribe May later added a famous graffito in regnal year 30 of Amenophis III.[31]   But probably the most interesting of such enterprises was the building of a sanctuary to Sekhmet within the mortuary temple of Sahure at Abusir, evidently as early as the reign of Tuthmosis III.[32]   It is beyond credence that the architect and craftsmen who erected this shrine would have been entirely unaffected by the subject matter if not the style of the adjacent Old Kingdom reliefs. It is perhaps significant in this connection that the only reliefs of kings known to the writer in which the muscles of the neck are delineated are those of Sahure and Akhenaten[33] (Ills. 5 and 6).

The excavation of the great sphinx of Gizeh, which was correctly identified as representing the IVth Dynasty king Khephren, in the reign of Tuthmosis IV, was a spectacular investigation of an ancient monument in the XVIIIth Dynasty, though there had been some activity on this site earlier in the period.[34]   But doubtless the most notable, and from our point of view the most significant, of these archaeological enterprises was the search for the tomb of the god Osiris at Abydos.   The identification in the archaic cemetery there of the cenotaph of Djer, the second or third king of the Ist Dynasty, as the holy place in question was a fair deduction.   The peculiar character of the blue decorated pottery that Petrie found in the lowest levels of the mass of votive sherds that covered the site suggests that this identification was made in the reign of Amenophis III when there was marked increase of activity at Abydos.[35]

An inscription in the tomb of Kheruef, the High Steward of Queen Tiye, informs us that the celebration of the First Jubilee of Amenophis III was made in accordance with the records of olden times, and goes on to infer that the festival had not been so made since the time of the ancestors.[36]   Actually, earlier kings in the Dynasty, such as Tuthmosis III and Amenophis II had celebrated jubilees,[37] and there must have been

---

[26]Wildung (1969) p. 66, Dok. XVI, 70a.

[27]*Ibid.* Dok. XVI, 70b.

[28]Gardiner (1946) pp. 47-48.

[29]Porter & Moss (1927-74) III, rev. edn. pt. 1, p. 325.

[30]Wildung (1969) p. 142, Dok. XX, 400a.

[31]*Ibid.* Dok. XX, 400b.

[32]Borchardt (1910-13) I, p. 107ff.

[33]*Ibid.* II, pl. 17; Aldred (1973) No. 12.

[34]Wildung (1969) pp. 206-07.

[35]Petrie (1901) p. 17.

[36]Fakhry (1943) p. 492, 11.9-11 of text.

[37]Aldred (1967) pp. 1-6: for a contrary view, see Hornung-Staehelin (1974) p. 77.

enough precedents available to determine the correct observance of the rites in the reign of Amenophis III. The emphasis upon special research into earlier records underlines the intense antiquarian interest in such subjects during the reign of this king. Perhaps we may have an example of this research in the archaic design of the cloak which Amenophis III wore on this occasion;[38] and in the fragment of an early dynastic slate palette probably from Abydos and shared between Cairo and Brooklyn, which is carved on the obverse with part of a ceremonial scene, evidently an early example of the Jubilee rites, and on the reverse with part of the figures of Queen Tiye and Amenophis III. The latter scene may also well commemorate a jubilee ceremony.[39]

One of the pundits doubtless concerned in such a scrutiny of the ancient records was the sage Amenophis-son of-Hapu whose family rose to great importance during this reign. In Ptolemaic times he was deified as Amenothes a god of healing. He figures large in the jubilee scenes carved in relief on the walls of the temple which Amenophis III built at Sulb;[40] and his antiquarian leanings are shown in a statue of him from Karnak which breaks entirely with the stylistic conventions of his period and revives the features of the XIIIth Dynasty in its pose, costume, musclature, heavy-lidded eyes, and in the lined face with its introspective expression.[41] If it were not for the inscription, this piece would almost certainly be dated to the late Middle Kingdom.[42]

The evidence for an interest in the monuments of the Old Kingdom as a source of inspiration during the XVIIIth Dynasty seems to the writer established as a *prima facie* case, and worthy of fuller investigation. It still continued in the reign of Akhenaten. We have already mentioned the research undertaken for the celebration of the first jubilee of Amenophis III. If the writer is correct in his belief that this coincided with the first jubilee of the Aten under Akhenaten,[43] then some explanation is available for the extensive illustration of this rite in one of the temples built to the Aten at Karnak in the first years of the reign.[44] An important feature of the decoration of Old Kingdom temples from the time of Kheops onwards was the representation of the Sed Festival. At Karnak, Akhenaten is shown wearing similar costume, carrying similar sceptres and moving through similar shrines as Niuserre in the reliefs from his sun-templs at Abu Ghurab[45] (Ills. 7 and 8). Moreover it is noteworthy that with the sudden appearance of the revolutionary Karnak style of art under Akhenaten, his courtiers should be shown deferentially bowing low in the same posture adopted by the palace officials of Sahure, Niuserre, Wenis and Phiops II.[46] Perhaps it is not entirely a coincidence that the pose of an infant on the lap of an adult which appears in the Brooklyn statue of Phiops II and his mother, Queen Ankhnes-mery-re, should not be repeated until the reign of Akhenaten:[47] or the statuettes of Akhenaten and his queen holding hands should depart so radically from the conventions of royal standing statues in the XVIIIth Dynasty though they do recall a triad of King Mykerinus of the IVth Dynasty.[48] At least we receive more than an echo of the Old Kingdom at Amarna where three of the courtiers for this brief interlude revive the Old Kingdom title of *rekh nesut*, King's Acquaintance.[49]

This enhanced interest during the XVIIIth Dynasty in the classic past of the Old Kingdom, however, did not prevent the age from being one of innovation, particularly as a result of more intimate contacts with the world

[38]Aldred (1969) p. 74

[39]Bothmer (1964) pp. 1-4.

[40]Lepsius (1848-59) III, pl. 83b.

[41]Legrain (1906) I, No. 42127.

[42]*Cf.* Koefoed-Petersen (1950) pp. 18-19, No. 25.

[43]Aldred (1959) p. 19ff.

[44]Hornung-Staehelin (1974) pp. 36-37.

[45]Bissing (1905-28) II, pl. 16.

[46]*E.g.* Borchardt (1910-13) I, pls. 11, 32, 52.

[47]Bothmer-Keith (1974) pp. 30-31. An earlier version in the same tradition however, is the damaged statue of Hatshepsut in the lap of her nurse (Cairo, J.E. No. 56264).

[48]Aldred (1973) figs. 39-41.

[49]Davies (1903-08) I, pl. xxxvii; II, pls. viii, xx; V, p. 7.

of the Eastern Mediterranean. The new international social order based upon a chariot-using military caste with the king at its head did not repudiate the Egyptian past, but rather saw in it a vindication of its contemporary viewpoint. Akhenaten's claim to "live in truth" appears to be no more than an affirmation of the vaildity of the Egyptian cosmic system as at its first creation. These constraints kept the Egyptian artist well within the bounds of tradition. Egyptian art had grown up in the service of its kings and could not be fundamentally changed until a new conception of government prevailed. Though Akhenaten introduced into Egyptian religious thinking a more joyous acceptance of the natural world and a more rational belief in a universal sole god, he did not change any of the ideas of kingship. Indeed, under the influence of the sun cult he appears to have reverted to some concepts of the divinity of the Pharaoh that belong to very early times.[50] The Royal Family are represented on the monuments in precisely the same aspective manner as had come down from the Archaic Period when the forms of art were first established. Only some idiosyncratic distortions were introduced, undoubtedly at the insistence of Akhenaten himself, in the portrayal of the persons of the King, the Queen and their daughters.

There were, however, two aspects in which the art of the Amarna period differed fundamentally from the Pharaonic art which had preceded it. The sudden introduction of these innovations entitles us to regard it as revolutionary. The first concerning subject-matter was deliberate; the second concerning a new space-concept, was unconscious.

When Akhenaten proscribed the representation of his sun-god in iconic form, he banished at a stroke nearly all the traditional subjects that had been reserved for the decoration of temples since earliest times. Even when he felt obliged to preserve conventional themes, he gave them a new look. Thus the scene in which the Pharaoh frees Egypt from evil forces by dispatching the traditional foes before the god of the temple is changed to show the slaughtering being undertaken beneath the elaborated symbol of the new sun-god in the presence of the Queen and the eldest daughter[51] (Ill. 9).

This example, however, is almost the only one of the traditional subjects to be retained. In their place appear incidents from the life of the Royal Family such as one finds in the house stelae from Amarna. There were no precedents for such themes and the court artists had to create from scratch an iconography which would express the ideology of the new faith. For this they fell back upon equally novel departures from the traditional subjects that had been introduced into the Theban tomb-paintings of the Dynasty, where incidents in the life that was past or the eternal life to come were given a fresh gloss.[52]

Thus on a house stela in Berlin (Ill. 10) Ankhesenpaaten plays with Queen Nefertiti's ear-ornament in much the same way as the child of a peasant woman reaches up to pull her mother's hair in the painting in the tomb of Menna at Thebes.[53]

Such new subjects for illustration in the cult of the Aten, however, are unlikely to be the invention of the craftsmen who carved the simple house stelae. They are more probably the products of the master artists who designed the scenes that were selected by Akhenaten himself and destined for the decoration of palaces and temples and particularly the walls of the vanished inner courts of the Amarna temples. Though only scattered fragments have survived from such reliefs, we are able to reconstruct whole scenes from parallels in the Amarna tombs and from objects found in the tomb of Tutankhamun. Thus a fragment of the reliefs from the dismantled temples of the Aten at Tell el-Amarna, excavated at Hermopolis and now in the Schimmel

---

[50]Aldred (1971) p. 6.

[51]Aldred (1973) p. 67.

[52]Mekhitarian (1954) p. 53ff.

[53]Ibid. p. 79.

collection is not easily capable of interpretation without a complete version found in the tomb of Tutankhamun, where the carved ivory appliqué on a box shows the scene of the King shooting at duck and fish in a pool.[54]

But the attractive domestic nature of these new icons should not obscure their fundamental religious import. The back-panel of the lion throne of Tutankhamun, for instance, made at the very end of the Amarna period and showing Queen Ankhesenpaaten annointing her husband, who wears the triple Atef-crown of his coronation, recalls in its composition and sentiment a relief in a late tomb at Tell el-Amarna of Nefertiti waiting upon Akhenaten.[55] To describe both icons as representing a vernacular and domestic scene, however, is to miss their proper significance. A comparison with the side panels of the throne of Tuthmosis IV in Boston and New York[56] will show that king seated upon his throne in the presence of Thoth and the lion-headed Weret-Hekau, the Great Enchantress, a goddess particularly associated with the royal crowns and with Isis, the personified throne. The scenes on both thrones show the Pharaoh being attended by the goddess of coronation, in the one case Isis-weret-hekau, in the other by the royal heiress Ankhesenpaaten in whom Tutankhamun's right to the throne lay.

The small gold-covered shrine from the tomb of Tutankhamun is a keypiece in preserving for us in the scenes with which it is embellished an idea of the decoration of the inner walls of the Amarna temples with the theme of the daily life of the royal pair as a significant rite.[57] It is noteworthy that despite the domestic nature of nearly all the reliefs, the shrine apparently housed a statue of the king as the god incarnate, while the queen, described as the Lady of the Palace, is also referred to as the Great Enchantress, doubtless identifying her with Isis-weret-hekau.[58]

As many observers have pointed out, Akhenaten was not averse to claiming a considerable share of the Aten's godhead and that share sometimes approached complete identity. But until very recently it has passed without comment that Nefertiti, too, is also a great divinity.[59] She alone makes offerings to the Aten on a par with the king and it is only this royal pair that the life-giving rays of the Aten sustain. On the Berlin house stela she sits on a royal throne while he is content with a simpler stool.[60] In the pair of statuettes in London and Paris, it is she who holds the king's hand.[61] She usually appears in a tall blue crown which seems to have been chosen to match the *khepresh* or "war crown" so often worn by her husband. In the earlier years of the reign, at least she is represented as an eminently desirable woman according to an Oriental ideal of attractiveness (Ill. 11); and this degree of allure is emphasised by the epithets that are frequently applied to her—"Fair of Face, Mistress of Joy, Endowed with Favours, Great of Love". There seems little doubt that like her husband she is to be regarded as a deity, in her case as a Venus figure.[62]

The Aten as the Heavenly Father had assimilated all the sun-gods and masculine principles in the Egyptian pantheon. While he is sometimes regarded as the mother and father of mankind, he remains a distinctly male concept, a sole god, a king in jubilee, lord of heaven and earth. The great female divinity who had existed since prehistoric times as a pervading influence in Egyptian religious thought, and had manifested herself as the primordial mother-wife-lover in such aspects as Nut, Hathor, Isis, Mut, Sekhmet, Amunet, etc., was notably lacking in the new sun-cult. As recently as the earlier part of the reign of Amenophis III a great temple to

---

[54]Aldred (1973) No. 150; Edwards (1972) No. 21.

[55]Carter (1923-31) I, pl. ii; Davies (1903-08) II, pl. xxxii.

[56]Hayes (1959) fig. 84.

[57]Edwards (1972) No. 25.

[58]*Ibid.*

[59]Wilson (1973) pp. 235ff.

[60]Aldred (1973) No. 16.

[61]See Note 48.

[62]Aldred (1973) p. 20.

the mother goddess Mut had been built at Karnak and furnished with hundreds of statues of the goddess. It is perhaps as something instinctive and subconscious, therefore, that Nefertiti with her children takes on the role of the divine female counterpart.

The XVIIIth Dynasty had seen a growth in the worship of deities grouped into trinities consisting of a god, his consort and their offspring. This characteristic was to become dominant in the later cults of Egypt; and the idea was not suppressed by the Aten religion, but rather transformed into the worship of the Royal Family. It is this family that is the focal point in the daily worship that was conducted by private persons in the chapels of their houses at Tell el-Amarna. The ostensibly informal and secular nature of the themes illustrated on the house stelae should not conceal from us that it is the subject-matter of a new cult, concerned with the significant domestic acts of a Holy Family who are the visible intermediaries between man and the godhead supreme, the invisible sun-god.

While historians have tended to stress the human and secular aspects of these new icons of the Aten religion, and to ignore that they replace the images of the old ruling gods with representations of the new divine rulers, there is yet a second and more subtle characteristic of Amarna art which has been almost entirely overlooked but which gives it a truly revolutionary significance.

If we examine the Berlin house stela for instance a little more closely we shall become aware that new trends are subverting the old traditional aspective view of reality. Even the Karnak talatat had adhered to the time-honoured canon of representing human feet as though they were seen in their interior aspect; and each pair of hands often as duplicates of the same hand. In place of these mere symbols of feet and hands, the Berlin stela carefully distinguishes the left and right feet, and the hands of the children also appear to be different-iated though the scale is too small for certainty. What is clear, however, is that while the side-lock of Meketaten is shown in detail worn on her right side, those of the other children are obscured since they are facing left. In other words, the artist conceived of his figures as existing within the reality of space and not within the two dimensional confines of the picture area.[63]

This is an entirely new vision on the part of the sculptor which is rare in the ancient world before this time. Admittedly in that vernacular art which is particularly evident in the Theban wall-paintings, left and right feet had appeared as an artistic aberration, at least as early as the tomb of Djeserkaresonb, but such occurrences are only sporadic.[64] Thus, one scene of guests at meat from the tomb of Nebamun in the British Museum distinguishes between left and right feet whereas its companion painting from the same tomb makes no such discrimination.[65] The distinction between left and right feet is not made in the carefully sculptured tombs of Khaemhet, Surer and Kheruef dating to the last years of Amenophis III; nor does it appear in the Theban tombs of Parennefer and Ramose dating to the first years of the reign of Akhenaten. It puts in a tentative appearance on the Boundary Stelae at Tell el-Amarna, and is fully established on the Berlin stela and the carved slab from the Royal Tomb, the latter both dating to the period between Years 6 and 9 of the reign of Akhenaten.[66] It appears to be an innovation of the King's sculptors because it is confined to figures of the Royal Family. For others the old conventions prevailed, as is evident on the walls of the private tombs at Tell el-Amarna.

As with feet, so with hands. It is sometimes difficult to decide whether a left or right hand has been correctly drawn on the same body owing to the fact that a mere line defining the ball of the thumb is all that is required to differentiate one from the other. From the early Old Kingdom, the artist had distinguished a clenched right

---

[63]*Ibid.* p. 72.

[64]Mekhitarian (1954) p. 79.

[65]B.M. Regn. Nos. 37984, 37986.

[66]Aldred (1973) fig. 34, No. 16.

hand from a clenched left hand, though he did not always correctly represent them on the same figure, especially when it was shown facing left.[67] In the Amarna Period, however, there is frequently an effort exhibited to look at hands with a fresh vision and to represent them properly in a spatial context. Sometimes the result is a little naive, as in a relief of Akhenaten wringing the neck of a sacrificial duck, where the artist has attempted to give a twisting motion to the right hand.[68] But other essays are more successful, such as the fingers of the harpist and lutenists in the orchestra that provides incidental music for the royal feast. The relief in the Schimmel Collection showing an elegant mannerist hand dropping a lump of incense on the altar reveals a fresh observation alike of a novel scene and of the moment when the fingers open to release their burden.[69] This is an unmistakable right hand, seen with the fingers in recession.

But the relief, also in the Schimmel Collection (Ill. 12), showing a hand, probably that of Akhenaten himself, holding up an olive branch bending under the weight of its fruit to the caressing rays of the Aten is the best testimony to the spatial reality of the new vision.[70] The scene is unique. The olive, an exotic tree imported into Egypt in the New Kingdom, has here replaced the traditional bouquets that are offered to the Aten. The novelty of the scene may have induced the artist to draw the branch and the hand that holds it from life and not according to time-honoured convention. The grasping hand is drawn to show the thumb in relation to the branch and the enclosing fingers in an aspect which as nearly approached perspective as any Egyptian draughtsman ever attained. The contrast between the old and the new will be apparent by comparing the hand of the king in this relief with those of the Aten rays.

The view of such a hand drawn as though operating within a spatial reality necessarily involved the artist in attempting to give an illusion of depth within the confines of the scene he was representing in relief or painting. An example of this is the relief showing a stand of wheat, again in the Schimmel Collection[71] (Ill. 13). In place of the conventional zone of ripened grain with ears in a uniform horizontal band, such as one finds in reliefs of the Old Kingdom and which recurred with little variation in harvest scenes of Dynasty XVIII, we see here an informal arrangement of bearded ears moving in the breeze. The heights of stalks and lengths of ears are varied to form a subtle rhythm interrupted by a few sword-like leaves. The effect, whether intentional or not, gives an illusion of depth; as though the spectator were looking through the moving stalks to what lies beyond and not at an impenetrable wall of straw.

A similar effect of depth is achieved in another relief showing part of an arbour (Ill. 14), evidently similar to that pictured on an ivory plaque in the Louvre.[72] The trunk of the vine climbs up part of the arbour; the branches are more lightly carved, and the veined leaves are even more faintly indicated, some of them so delicately as to seem to recede into the background. By contrast the grape clusters are boldly carved, giving weight and volume to the ripened fruit. The sculptor has shown here not only his delight in texture, but also his skill in suggesting depth by spatial relationships between different parts of the growing vine.

This novel conception of space in Egyptian art is seen in the reliefs carved on the walls of the tomb chapels at Tell el-Amarna, which almost certainly copied scenes used in the decoration of the Aten temples. Instead of the traditional extracts from pattern-books selected according to the taste of the patron and represented in a juxtaposition of different subjects, each wall is considered as a single unit and covered with a complete scene. In a chamber in the Royal Tomb one subject is spread over two adjacent walls, and the same arrangement is used in the private tombs at Tell el-Amarna, such as those of Meryre I and Mahu.[73]

---

[67]Schäfer (1974) pp. 297-99.

[68]Aldred (1973) No. 118.

[69]*Ibid.* No. 147.

[70]*Ibid.* No. 146.

[71]*Ibid.* No. 93.

[72]*Ibid.* No. 83.

[73]Davies (1903-08) I, pls. i, x, xxv; IV, pls. xiv, xx-xxii, xxiv-xxvi.

What is noteworthy in these scenes is that the vertical line defining the corner where two adjacent walls meet has been entirely ignored, whereas in the Theban tombs of the Dynasty, the division is emphasised by a twisted rope pattern and block borders.[74] In other words, at Tell el-Amarna the Egyptian artist was now conceiving of space as a totality and not as the contiguity of separate if adjacent planes.

The same management of space but in its exterior aspects is seen in the sarcophagi of the period. Tutankhamun has a sarcophagus with one of the goddesses of the four quarters standing at each exterior corner in such a position that half her body falls vertically on the long side and the other half on the short end.[75] This is the persistence of a new design which was introduced in the Amarna period to judge from a fragment in Berlin in which Nefertiti plays the part of a goddess.[76] That this was outside the natural experience of the Egyptian artist is suggested by the sarcophagi of Ay and Haremheb which although a mere five years or so later in date, show that the position of the goddesses has been shifted so that two are fully revealed on each long side, only their winged arms being visible at the head and foot ends, and so conforming more comfortably to Egyptian instincts.[77] That the Tutankhamun sarcophagus was no artistic sport is seen in the same disposition of the goddesses at the corners of the alabaster canopic chest which contained the King's viscera.[78]

Even more significant is the design of the statues of these same goddesses who stand with arms outstretched to protect the gilded shrine enclosing the chest.[79] Three of them have their heads turned to the right while Selkis looks to her left (Ill. 15). It is therefore not possible to place these figures in their proper guardian stations without directing their gaze around three sides of the chest. The Egyptian designer has used them to encircle the square, a reversal of his usual practice of squaring the circle.

This new conception of space breaks out of the Egyptian artistic consciousness only in these somewhat oblique manifestations. Beneath the surface of Amarna art, a new idea of representing the space around them prevailed for a brief moment in the vision of the artists of the Egyptian Court; and as such it was a notable achievement in the art of the Late Bronze Age.

References

ALDRED, C.

1959   "The Beginning of the El 'Amarna Period." *Journal of Egyptian Archaeology* 45 (1959) pp. 19ff.

1961   *New Kingdom Art in Ancient Egypt, 1570-1320 B.C* 2nd edn. London

1967   "The Second Jubilee of Amenophis II." *Zeitschrift für Ägyptische Sprache & Altertumskunde* 94 (1967) pp. 1ff.

1969   "The 'New Year' Gifts to the Pharaoh." *Journal of Egyptian Archaeology* 55 (1969) pp. 73ff.

1971   *Egypt: The Amarna Period and the End of the Eighteenth Dynasty.* Cambridge Ancient History, rev. edn. fasc. 71. Cambridge.

1973   *Akhenaten and Nefertiti.* London.

---

[74]Vandier (1952-69) IV, p. 14.

[75]Carter (1923-31) II, pl. LXV.

[76]Schäfer (1931) pl. 56

[77]Hornung (1971) pls. 62-65.

[78]Carter (1923-31) III, pl. X.

[79]*Ibid.* pls. VII, VIII.

BISSING, W. VON.
  1905-28 *Das Re-Heiligtum des Königs Ne-Woser-Re (Rathures)*. 3 vols. Berlin & Leipzig.

BISSON DE LA ROQUE.
  1937 B(isson de la) R(oque), (F). Fouilles de l'Institut français d'archéologie orientale du Caire, T. XVII. *Tod (1934 à 1936)*. Cairo.

BORCHARDT, L.
  1910-13 *Das Grabdenkmal des Königs Sa3hu-Re'*. 3 vols. Leipzig.

BORCHARDT, L.
  1938 *Ägyptische Tempel mit Umgang*. Cairo.

BOTHMER, B.V.
  1969 "A New Fragment of an Old Palette." *Journal of the American Research Center in Egypt* 8 (1969) pp. 1ff.

BOTHMER, B.V. & KEITH, J.
  1974 *Brief Guide to the Department of Egyptian and Classical Art*. The Brooklyn Museum, New York.

CARTER, H.
  1923-31 *The Tomb of Tut.ankh.Amen*. 3 vols. London.

DAVIES, N. DE G.
  1903-08 *The Rock Tombs of El Amarna*. 6 vols. Egypt Exploration Society, Archaeological Survey of Egypt. *Memoirs* 13-18. London

DERCHAIN, P.
  1966 "Réflexions sur la Décoration des Pylônes." *Bulletin de la Société française d'Egyptologie* 46 (1966) pp. 17ff.

EDWARDS, I.E.S.
  1972 *Treasures of Tutankhamun*. (Catalogue of the Tutankhamun Exhibition held in the British Museum) London.

FAKHRY, A.
  1943 "A Note on the Tomb of Kheruef at Thebes." *Annales du Service des Antiquités de l'Egypte* 42 (1943) pp. 449ff.

FAZZINI, R.
  1975 *Images for Eternity: Egyptian Art from Berkeley & Brooklyn*. The Brooklyn Museum, New York.

GARDINER, A.
  1946 "Davies's Copy of the Great Speos Artemidos Inscription." *Journal of Egyptian Archaeology* 32 (1946) pp. 136ff.

HASSAN, S.
  1955 "The Causeway of Wnis at Sakkara." *Zeitschrift für Ägyptische Sprache und Altertumskunde* 80 (1955) pp. 136ff.

HAYES, W.
  1959 *The Scepter of Egypt*. Part 2. Cambridge, Mass. 1959.
  1962 *Egypt: Internal Affairs from Tuthmosis I to the Death of Amenophis III*. Cambridge Ancient History, rev. edn. fasc. 10. Cambridge.

HORNUNG, E.
  1971 *Das Grab des Haremhab im Tal der Könige*. Berne.

HORNUNG, E., STAEHELIN, E., ET AL.
  1974 Studien zum Sedfest (Aegyptiaca Helvetica I) Geneva.

JAMES, T.
  1965 *Egypt: From the Expulsion of the Hyksos to Amenophis I*. Cambridge Ancient History, rev. edn. fasc. 34. Cambridge.

JEQUIER, G.
  1936-40 *Le Monument Funéraire de Pepi II*. 3 vols. Cairo.

KOEFOED-PETERSEN, O.

1950   *Catalogue des Statues et Statuettes Egyptiennes.* Glyptothèque Ny Carlsberg, Publication No. 3 . Copenhagen.

LACAU, P.

1909   *Stèles du Nouvel Empire.* Cairo, Musée des Antiquités Egyptiennes, *Catalogue Général* Cairo.

LEGRAIN, G.

1906   *Statues and Statuettes des rois et particuliers* vol. 1. Cairo, *Musée* des Antiquités Egyptiennes, *Catalogue Général* Cairo.

LEPSIUS, R.

1848-59 *Denkmaeler aus Aegypten und Aethiopien.* 6 vols. Berlin.

MEKHITARIAN, A.

1954   *Egyptian Painting.* Trans. by S. Gilbert. Great Centuries of Painting. Geneva.

MOND, R. & MYERS, O.

1940   *Temples of Armant.* 2 vols. London.

NAVILLE, E.

1894-1908 *The Temple of Deir el Bahari.* 7 vols. London.

PETRIE, W.

1901   *Royal Tombs of the Earliest Dynasties.* Pt. II. London.

PIANKOFF, A.

1964   "Les compositions théologiques du nouvel empire égyptien." *Bulletin de l'Institut français d'archéologie orientale du Caire* 62 (1964) pp. 121ff.

PORTER, B. & MOSS, R.

1927-74 *Topographical Bibliography of Ancient Egyptian Hieroglyphic Texts, Reliefs, & Paintings.* 7 vols. Oxford.

REDFORD, D.

1967   *History and Chronology of the Eighteenth Dynasty of Egypt.* Toronto.

REYMOND, E.

1969   *The Mythical Origin of the Egyptian Temple.* Manchester.

SCHÄFER, H.

1931   *Amarna in Religion und Kunst.* Leipzig.

1974   *Principles of Egyptian Art.* ed. E. Brunner-Traut. Trans and Edited by J. Baines. Oxford.

SMITH, W.S.

1965   *The Art and Architecture of Ancient Egypt.* 2nd edn. Harmondsworth.

VANDIER, J.

1952-69 *Manuel d'Archéologie Egyptienne* 5 vols. Paris.

WILDUNG, D.

1969   *Die Rolle Ägyptischer Könige in Bewusstsein ihrer Nachwelt* I. Berlin.

WILSON, J.

1973   "Akh-en-Aton and Nefert-iti." *Journal of Near Eastern Studies* 32 (1973) pp. 235ff.

PLATES

Ill. 1. Jarmo: Spheres, Discs, Cones, Tetrahedrons;
Prehistoric Project. Oriental Institute, University of Chicago.

UR

Ill. 2. Ur: Incised Discs;
University Museum, University of Pennsylvania.

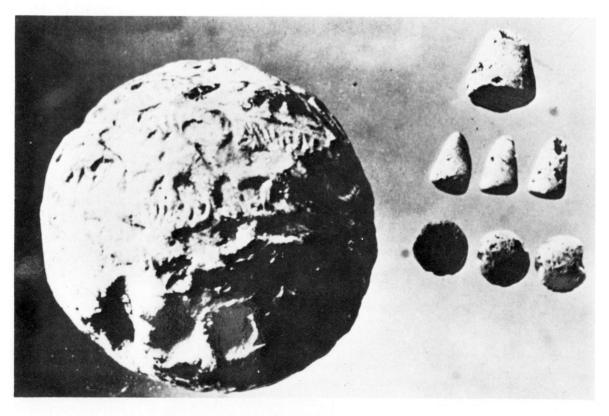

Ill. 3. Susa: Bulla with its content of abnati.
Departement des Antiquités Orientales, Musée du Louvre, Paris, France.

Ill. 4. Susa: Bulla with check marks indicating the number and shapes of abanati inside;
Département des Antiquités Orientales, Musée du Louvre, Paris, France.

Ill. 5. Numerical Clay Tablet;
The Oriental Institute, The University of Chicago.

Ill. 6. Archaic Tablet;
The Babylonian Collection, Yale University.

Ill. 1. Detail of scribe. Mastaba of Sekhem-ankh-ptah.
Dynasty 5. Courtesy of Museum of Fine Arts, Boston.

Ill. 2. Detail of field-hands. Mastaba of Sekhem-ankh-ptah.
Dynasty 5. Courtesy of Museum of Fine Arts, Boston.

Ill. 1.   Resheph Stela.

26.645

Ill. 2. Ivory strips from el-Jisr.

32.2711

Ill. 3. Bone strip with running fawn.
From Tell Beit Mirsim.

Ill. 4. Cylinder seal from Ugarit.

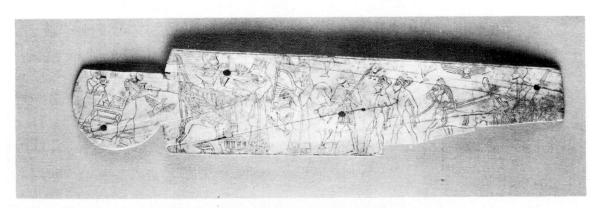

Ill. 5. Military and feast scene from Megiddo VIIA.

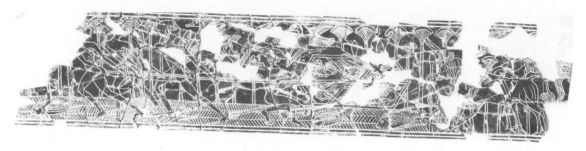

Ill. 6.   Hunting for provisions, ivory from Tell el-Fara (South).

Ill. 7.   Feast scene, ivory from Tell el-Fara (South).

Ill. 8.   Samaria ivory.

Ill. 1. Conical shaped rocks in Japanese Dry Garden.

Ill. 2. Great Pyramids.

Ill. 3. Lotus Bundle.

Ill. 4. Papyriform with triangular stem.

Ill. 5. Capitals illustrating different types of vegetation.

Ill. 7. Hieroglyphic Group meaning Egypt.

Ill. 6. God of Gardens, Khem.

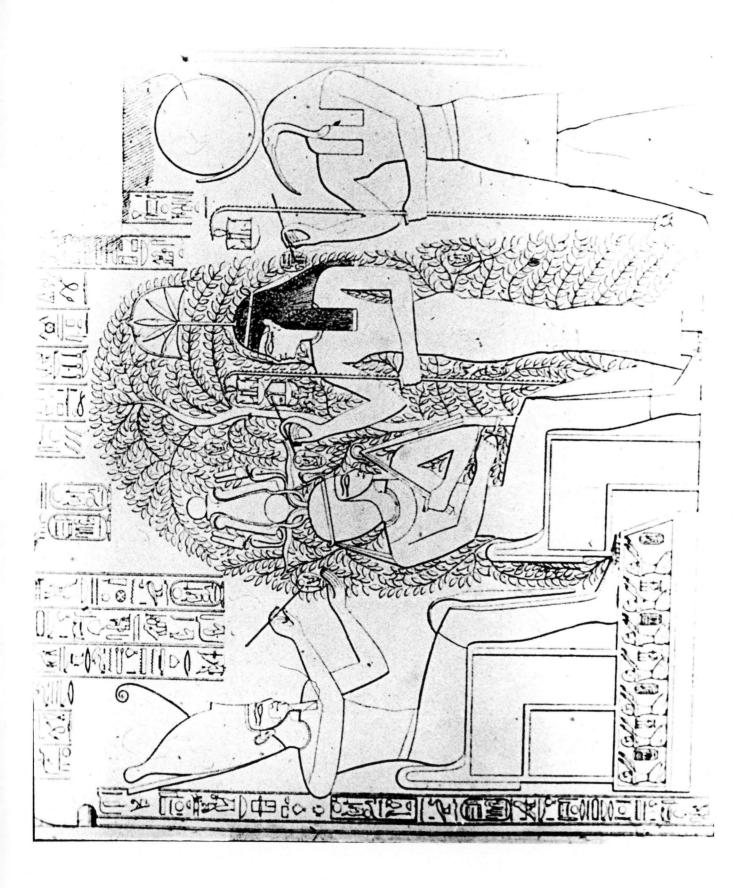

Ill. 9. Garden in front of Tomb.

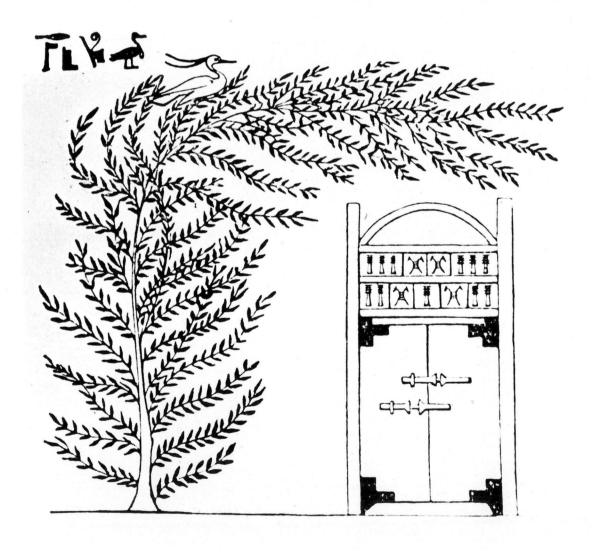

Ill. 10. Tomb of Osiris with Tamarisk.

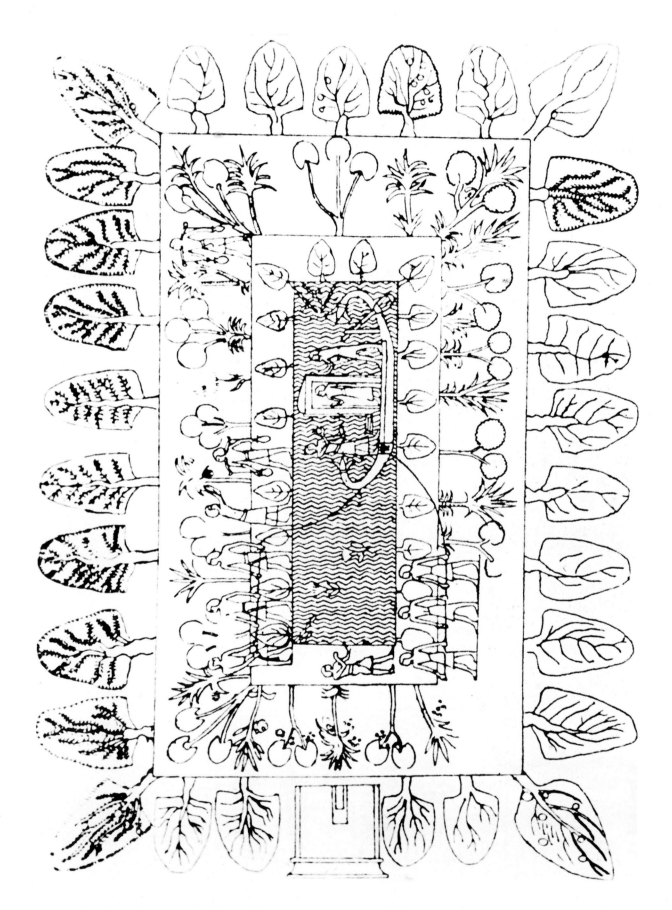

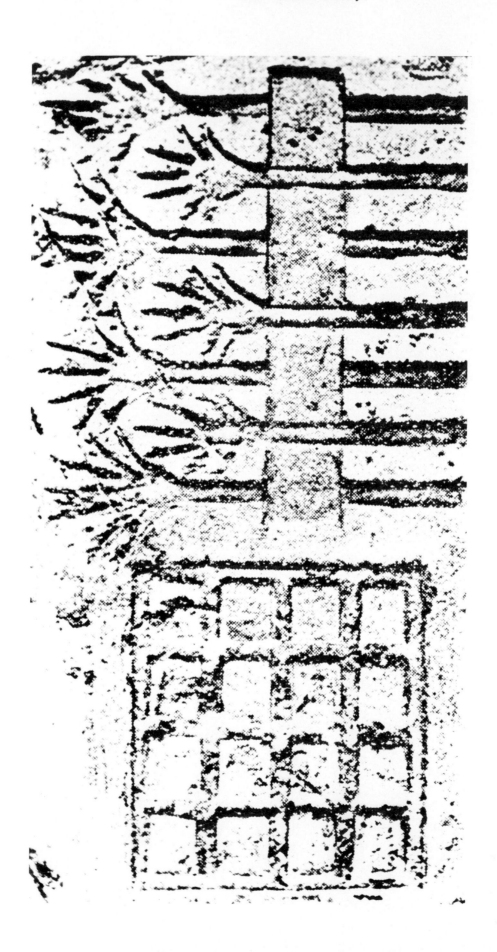

Ill. 13. Reconstructed birdseye view of Estate of High Official.

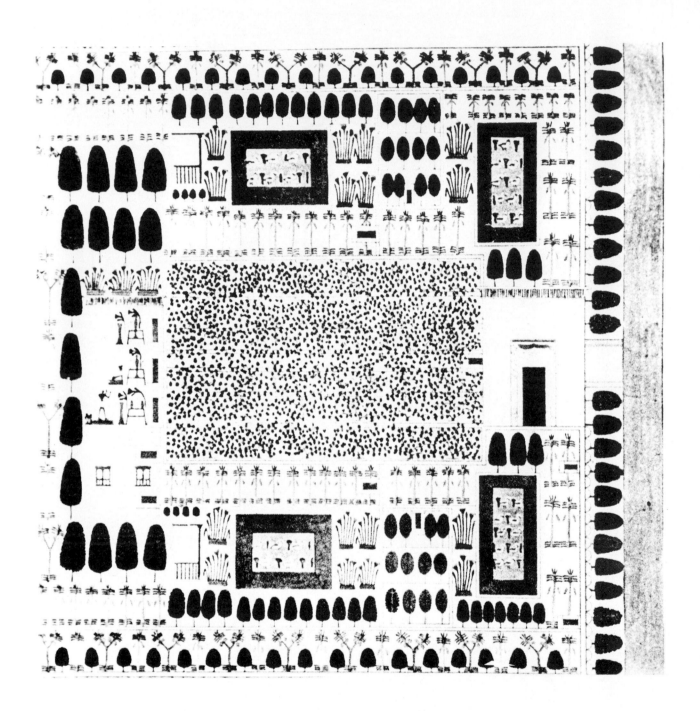

Ill. 14. Estate of High Official.

Ill. 15. Date Palm.

Ill. 16. Monkey Picking Figs.

Ill. 18. Flowers on floor as decoration.

Ill. 17. Pomegranate.

Ill. 19.   Offering of flowers.

Ill. 20.   Visitors being received in garden.

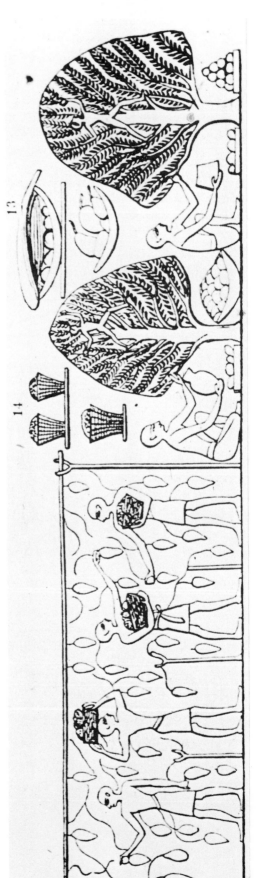

Ill. 21. Vine arbour supported by forked pillar.

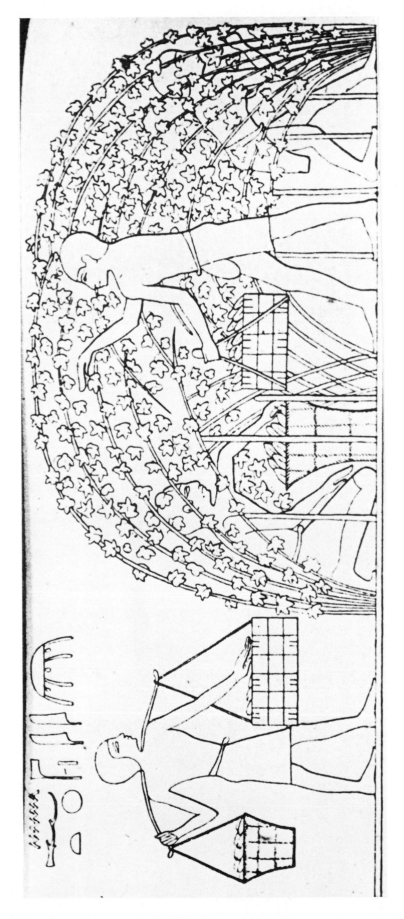

Ill. 22. Round vine arbour.

Ill. 23.   Elaborate trellis with supports.

Ill. 24.   Watering device.

Ill. 25. Watering device shown in garden of Apoui at Thebes.

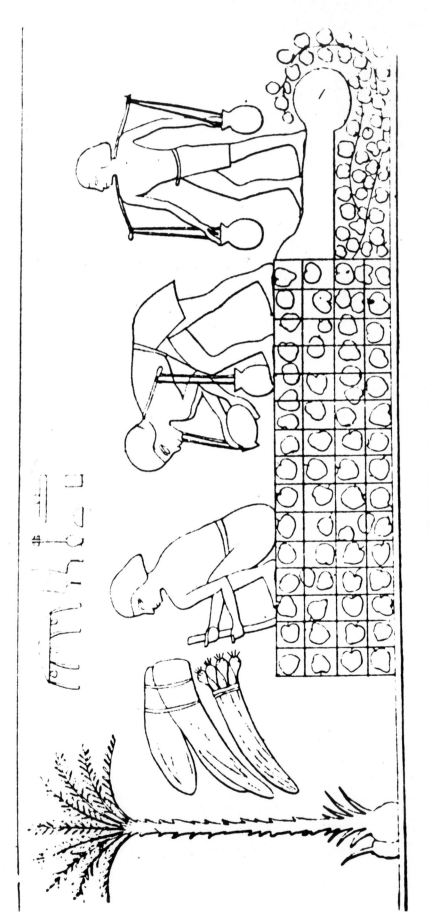

Ill. 26. Vegetable garden.

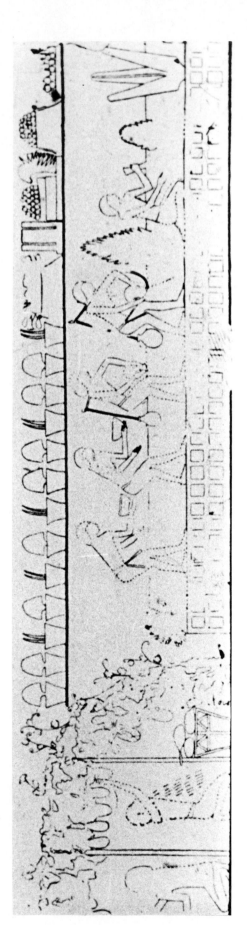

Ill. 27. Potted plants in garden at el-Bersheh.

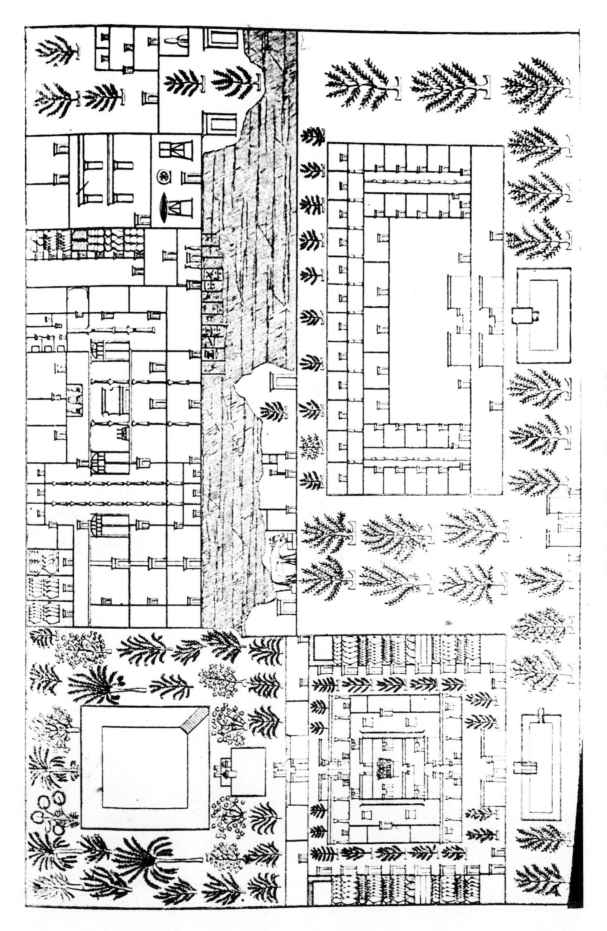

Ill. 28. The Palace of Merire, High Priest.

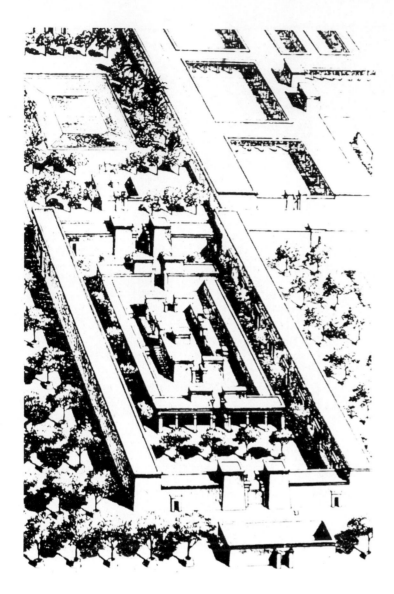

Ill. 29
Palace of Merire.
Suggested restoration of Royal Villa.

Ill. 30.
Trees in individual beds.

Ill. 31. Small residential dwelling with garden.

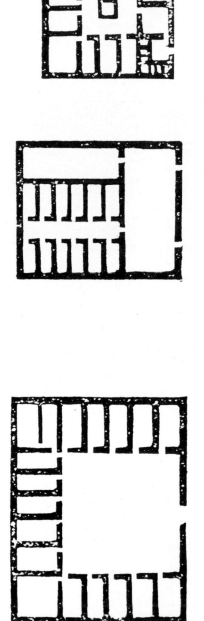

Ill. 32. Houses surrounding courtyard.

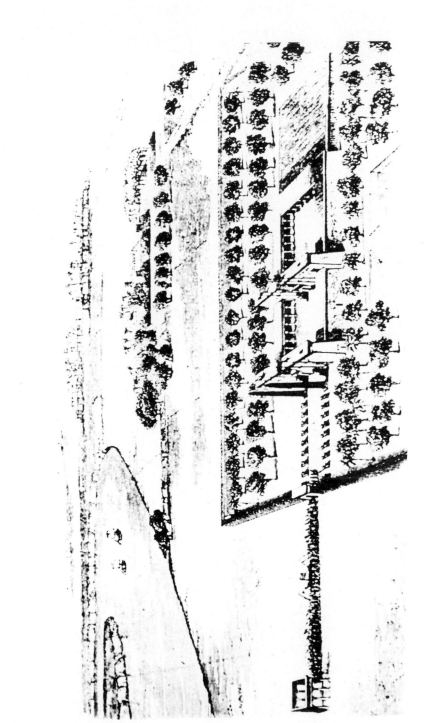

Ill. 33. Temple garden.

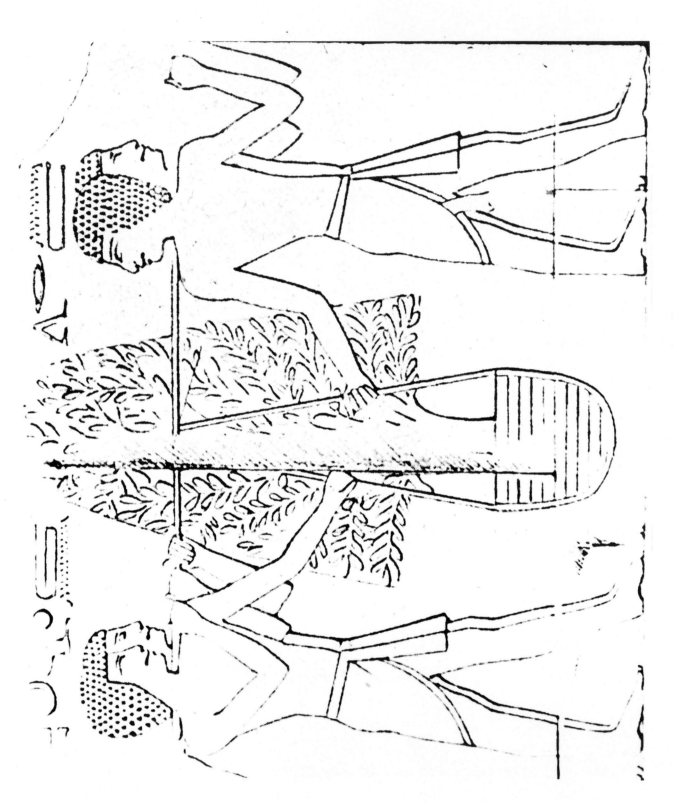

Ill. 35. Transporting the trees from Punt.

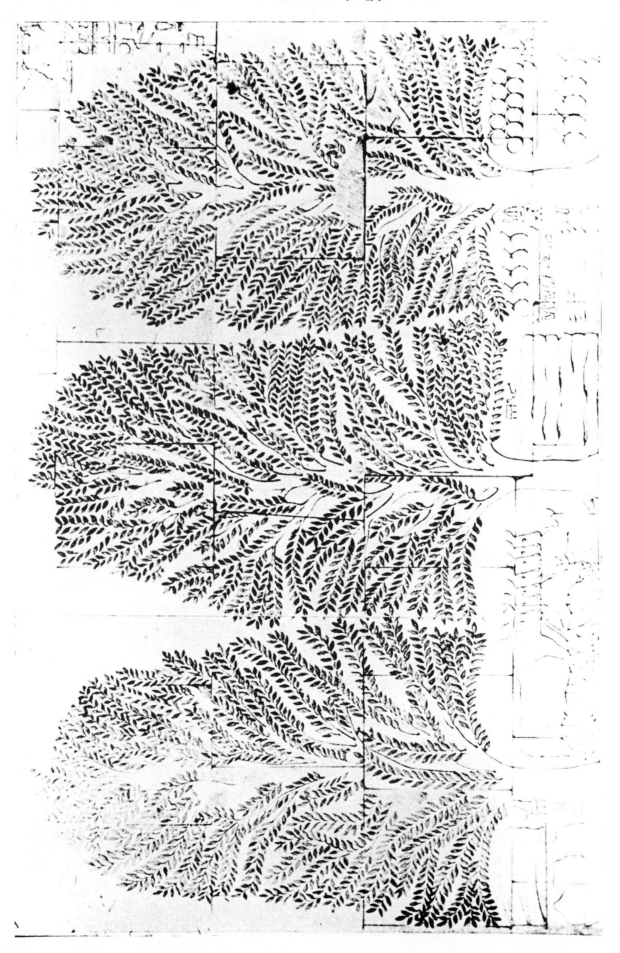

Ill. 36. Cattle feeding under trees.

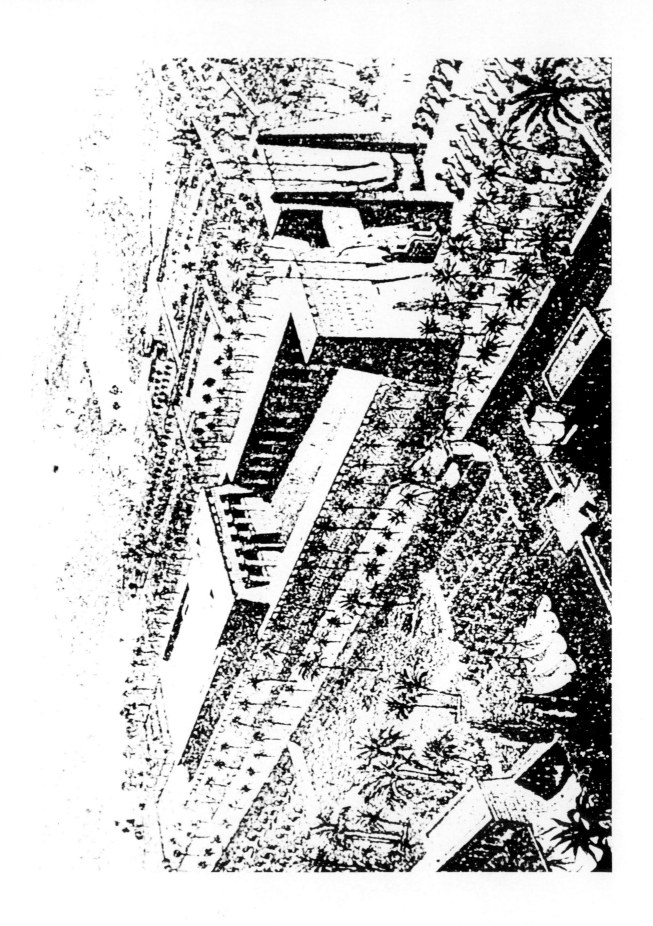

Ill. 37. Temple surrounded by trees.

34.002 (1)

Ill. 1. Stela of Amosis (upper part): limestone from Abydos.

Ill. 2.
Relief of Tanent and Mont crowning Nebhepetre:
Limestone from Tod.

Ill. 3.
Model relief of Akhenaten.

Ill. 4.
Relief of Sahure:
Limestone from Abusir.

Ill. 5.
Jubilee Scene with Akhenaten.

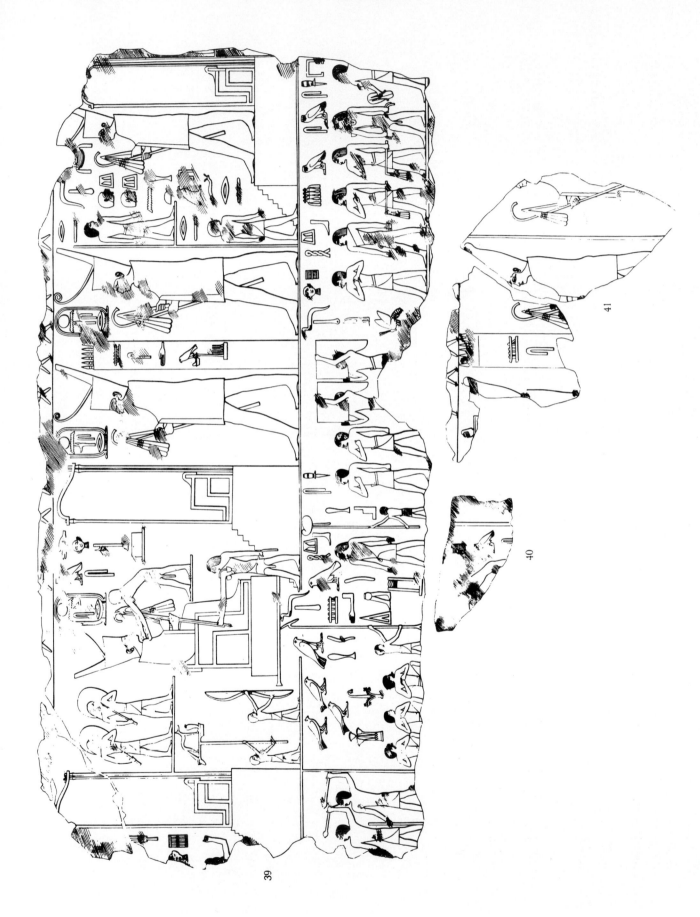

Ill. 6. Jubilee relief of Niuserre: Limestone from Abu Ghurab.

Ill. 7.   Akhenaten slaying an asiatic—detail from the royal barge.

Ill. 8.   The Royal Family.

Ill. 10.   Offering of an olive-branch.

Ill. 9. Torso of Queen Nefertiti.

Ill. 11.   Stand of wheat.

Ill. 12.   Arbour with vine.

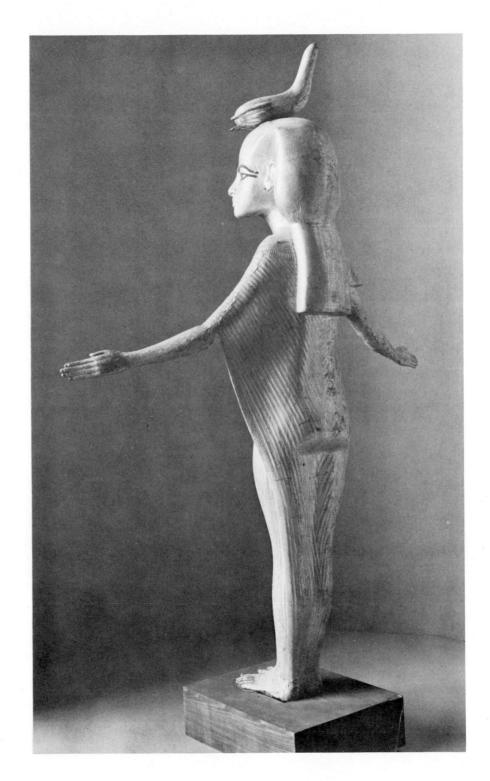

Ill. 13. The Goddess Selkis.